Cyril G. Hopkins, Perry G. Holden

The Sugar Beet in Illinois

Cyril G. Hopkins, Perry G. Holden

The Sugar Beet in Illinois

ISBN/EAN: 9783337130701

Printed in Europe, USA, Canada, Australia, Japan

Cover: Foto ©Andreas Hilbeck / pixelio.de

More available books at **www.hansebooks.com**

UNIVERSITY OF ILLINOIS,

Agricultural Experiment Station.

URBANA, JANUARY, 1898.

BULLETIN No. 49.

THE SUGAR BEET IN ILLINOIS.

The results of experiments and investigations by the Experiment Station to determine the possibilities of the Beet Sugar Industry for Illinois show:

1. That Illinois can produce sugar beets of excellent quality for manufacturing purposes.

2. That this production is not limited to particular soils or sections of the state.

3. That Illinois possesses many advantages for the development of the industry such as good soil, plenty of fuel, lime rock and pure water, besides good markets and the best of transportation.

4. That under present conditions beets can be produced at a cost which will insure comparatively large profits for both grower and manufacturer.

5. That accurate knowledge of the practical details of the work and coöperation between grower and manufacturer are absolutely essential to success.

WHAT THE EXPERIMENT STATION HAS DONE.

It conducted experiments last year that show without doubt that Illinois can excel in the beet sugar industry whenever its citizens choose to undertake it seriously. It sent a trusty employé to the fields and factories of Nebraska to collect detailed information upon the growth of the crop, the profits of the business, the organization and starting of the enterprise, and the dangers and difficulties that experience has discovered. It has brought into this bulletin, so far as space would permit, all the information and counsel possible, and it does not hesitate to recommend the business to the people of the state as an industry that is exceedingly profitable, nor to say that now is a favorable time to start.

Acknowledgments are due to the management at both Grand Island and Norfolk factories for courtesies extended to our representative and to the numerous individuals and companies that have contributed to the value of this publication by furnishing detailed information and by loan of cuts of special machinery.

That portion of the bulletin including analysis of samples grown in this state was prepared by Mr. C. G. Hopkins, who personally conducted all analyses, and the rest was prepared by Professor P. G. Holden, who has in charge the general subject of sugar beet experimentation.

What the Experiment Station Proposes to Do.

From now on the locality is the unit for purposes of experimentation. Communities should organize, remembering that it would take fifty good factories to manufacture the sugar consumed by the citizens of Illinois, for which they pay annually some twelve million dollars. It has cost the Station much time, effort, and money to show that Illinois is by nature a sugar producing state and to point out the principles essential to success, and this work cannot be repeated. No general distribution of beet seed, therefore, will again be made, neither does the law permit analyses for private individuals. There are, however, many local questions and matters of education in methods of beet culture and in the establishing of factories that are of fundamental importance to any community that is thinking of growing beets on a commercial scale. The Station desires to be helpful and proposes to coöperate with any locality or organization that is seriously interested and is willing to comply with the following conditions :

1. To secure an organization or some kind of union between not less than five citizens of the community within a radius of five miles from a common center.

2. To raise five trial fields of at least one-fourth acre each in representative soil and according to directions furnished by the Station.

3. To record data and collect samples as directed by the Station, and send them for analysis, transportation prepaid.

Communities desiring such assistance should arrange in advance upon the plan indicated above and at the earliest possible date. Seed will be supplied from here free of cost.

E. DAVENPORT,
Director.

CAN ILLINOIS PRODUCE SUGAR BEETS PROFITABLY AS A COMMERCIAL ENTERPRISE?

In the spring of 1897 high grade seed of the Original Klein Wanzleben variety, furnished by the United States Department of Agriculture, was sent with printed instructions for growing to 600 persons representing all sections of the state. Over 400 samples of beets from 64 counties of the state were returned to the Station during the months of October and November for analysis, and the tabulated results with brief explanations are given on the following pages. In studying these results it must be distinctly borne in mind that with very few exceptions the beets were grown by persons having no practical knowledge of the details of this peculiar industry, printed instructions being their only guide. It is to be regretted that, owing to lack of space, the full reports from the individuals growing the samples of beets, as to kind of soil, cultivation, etc., cannot accompany the analytical data, since they would readily explain many of the cases where low per cents. were obtained. Indeed the instances where beets received even normal treatment are the exception, rather than the rule. But this does not make the results obtained less valuable. If good beets can be produced under such conditions, there certainly can be little doubt as to the results when our farmers have become acquainted with the details of the industry. For marketable grades of beets see "Contract" on page 25.

Analytical Methods, Explanations of Terms, Etc.

In no case was a single beet analyzed, and as a rule, five or six beets were taken as a sample for analysis, the weight of the sample being taken after the beets had been washed and topped according to factory methods. The average weight was obtained by dividing the weight of the sample by the number of beets taken. The beets were then reduced to pulp and a large sample of the juice expressed.

The per cent. of solids in juice was obtained by means of standard Brix hydrometers, and the per cent. of sugar in juice was determined by the polariscope.

The purity coefficient means the per cent. of pure sugar in the total solid matter found in the juice, and is obtained by dividing the per cent. of sugar in the juice by the per cent. of solids in the juice.

For example, if the juice from a sample of beets contains 12 per cent. of sugar and 15 per cent. of solids its purity coefficent is 80; that is, in 100 pounds of the solid matter from the juice there are 80 pounds of sugar and 20 pounds of impurities. This is a very important matter, because the impurities are not only a total loss in themselves, but they have the effect of preventing the crystallization of about an equal amount of sugar, so that for the case in hand, it is possible to obtain only about 60 pounds of sugar instead of the 80 pounds which are present.

The per cent. of sugar in beets is found by multiplying the per cent. of sugar in juice by .95. This assumes the fresh beets to contain, as they do, an average of 95 per cent. of juice, although the percentage varies from about 94 per cent. to 96 per cent. It is thus possible to introduce an error of one or two-tenths per cent., which for the practical purposes of the work is insignificant, especially when we remember that the variation in different samples of beets carefully selected from the same plat is several times greater. (See tables 1 and 4).

These are the established analytical methods employed in beet sugar factories, and the results given are strictly comparable with analytical data from factories.

As a rule the size of the beets has a marked influence upon the percentage of sugar, the smaller beets having a high percentage of sugar and the larger beets a low percentage. This fact should always be borne in mind when studying tables of sugar beet analyses.

The true basis for sugar beet growers should be the highest yield of crystallizable sugar per acre. With beets much above two pounds average weight the percentage of sugar and the purity coefficient will be too low to secure the best results, while from beets of much less than one pound average weight the yield will be too low for the greatest profit, although the percentage of sugar and the purity coefficient may be high. In the following tables the most important data are, average weight of beets, per cent. of sugar in beets, and purity coefficient.

While all of the samples analyzed are reported in the following tables, it should be constantly borne in mind that samples of beets which give poor results are not necessarily evidence that good beets cannot be grown in the locality from which they came, or even on the same spot of ground. It is far more likely that the failure is due to ignorance or negligence as to the proper conditions and methods of growing sugar beets.

On the other hand samples which show a good quality are positive evidence that good beets can be grown in the locality from which they came.

Beets which were badly wilted when received were not analyzed. Several samples which were slightly wilted were analyzed. They are marked "wilted" in the tables. The effects of wilting are to decrease the weight of the beets and to increase the per cent. of sugar and solids. The purity coefficient is not affected.

In arranging the tables of results, the state is divided into the three general sections, northern, central and southern.

METEOROLOGICAL RECORDS, 1889–1897.

Temperature, Degrees, Fahrenheit.

	January.			February.			March.			April.		
	Mean.	Max.	Min.	Mean.	Max.	Min.	Mean.	Max.	Min.	Mean.	Max.	Min.
1889	29.28	57	-2	23.36	53	-7.5	39.92	72	18	51.9	75	25
1890	33.5	66	-5	34.66	68	7	33.35	61	2	52.32	81	29
1891	30.26	57	6	30.45	61	-9	32.55	65	-1	52.78	81	22
1892	19.2	57	-15	33	55	*	36.1	69	*	48.6	70.5	26
1893	14.8	48	*	25.8	51	*	37.8	76	*	49.3	75	30
1894	29.4	64	-21	24.7	58	-5	43.5	77	10	51.4	85	25
1895	19.5	57	-8	17.9	65	-20.5	35.9	84	7	52.3	88	27
1896	28.1	52	-5	29.6	68	-4	34.4	67	6	57.6	86	21
1897	22.3	59	-15	30.36	59	-2	39.77	66	20	48.4	79	21
Whole Period....	25.15	66	-21	27.76	68	-20.5	37.03	84	-1	51.62	88	21

	May.			June.			July.			August.		
	Mean.	Max.	Min.	Mean.	Max.	Min	Mean.	Max.	Min.	Mean.	Max.	Min.
1889	59.2	91	28	65.5	88	40	72.7	90.5	50	69.2	89	29.5
1890	58.27	87	33	74.56	96	47	73.02	97.5	45	68.74	96	44.5
1891	58.4	91	30	71.9	93	49	70.12	93	42	70.21	99	40
1892	57.9	82	36	70.6	94	51	73.3	96.5	46	71.5	94	47
1893	57.4	84	37	70.5	93	53	76.4	98	48	71.1	96	37
1894	59.6	89	32	73.4	97	34	73.8	98	47	72.3	99	41
1895	59.4	95	28	73.3	98.5	42	71.3	94	43	73.2	97	48
1896	68.2	91	45	70.2	92	49	73.8	95	49	72	97	44
1897	58	83	31	70	93	44	76	89	53	70	97	42
Whole Period....	59.59	95	28	71.11	98.5	34	73 38	98	42	70.92	99	29.5

	September.			October.			November.			December.		
	Mean.	Max	Min.	Mean.	Max.	Min.	Mean.	Max.	Min.	Mean.	Max.	Min.
1889	61.32	87.5	32	47.26	82	25	36.82	62	4	42.71	66	15
1890	60.46	89	33	52.07	76	27	42.62	68	21	30.91	58	8
1891	69.2	96	41	51.3	88.5	27	35.69	67	2	37	60	11
1892	63.9	87	42	53.6	88.5	19	34.8	64	7	27.7	60	-7
1893	66.5	97	31	53.3	84	18	37.3	75	6	30	63	-6
1894	65	94	38	51.9	84	28	35.9	67	12	32.9	59	-4
1895	67.7	94	32	45.9	75	12	38.2	73	4	31.1	59	-2
1896	61.9	91	30	48.8	79	24	39.9	74	9	33.3	62	8
1897	69.4	97.5	32	59.1	92	32	39.5	69	11	26.3	59	1
Whole Period....	65.04	97.5	30	51.47	92	12	37.86	75	2	32.44	66	-7

Rainfall, Inches.

	Jan	Feb.	Mar.	April.	May.	June.	July.	Aug.	Sept.	Oct.	Nov.	Dec.	Year.
1889	1.48	2.08	1.61	.61	5.52	6.81	5.81	.60	2.74	1.42	4.38	1.82	34.88
1890	5.26	1.87	2.70	4.11	3.56	3.80	2.83	1.93	1.19	2.35	1.63	.05	31.28
1891	.99	2.60	3.55	3.54	.89	2.08	1.41	2.86	.41	1.29	5.58	1.53	26.73
1892	.79	2.64	2.59	6.45	7.86	5.36	2.50	2.45	.93	.93	4.95	1.62	39.05
1893	1.05	4.48	3.20	7.68	4.83	1.55	.59	.06	3.62	1.14	2.98	1.09	32.37
1894	1.95	1.32	2.41	1.86	3.32	1.78	1.08	2.06	4.21	.51	2.77	1.44	24.72
1895	1.36	.52	.70	2.42	2.20	2.24	3.61	1.81	5.27	.21	3.07	5.71	29.12
1896	1.12	1.95	1.22	1.89	5.62	2.98	7.87	3.74	5.84	.42	2.87	.39	35.91
1897	4.53	1.17	4.10	3.65	1.80	5.15	4.68	.63	.31	.42	1.91	2.67	34.02
Ave...	2.06	2.07	2.45	3.58	3.95	3.53	3.37	1.79	2.72	.97	3.68	1.59	32.01

* Record incomplete.

TABLE I. RESULTS OF ANALYSES OF BEETS GROWN IN 1897.

One hundred and thirteen samples from eighteen counties of Northern Illinois.

County.	Town.	Grower.	Lab. No.	Planted.	Harvested.	Analyzed.	No. analyzed	Average weight, oz.	Per cent. Sugar in beets.	Per cent. Sugar in juice.	Per cent. Solids in juice	Purity coefficient.	Remarks.
Stephenson	Ridott	W. C. & L. M. Swanzey	246	May 4	Oct. 15	Oct. 22	6	19.8	**10.7**	11.3	16.1	**70.0**	Good cultivation.
Winnebago	Pecatonica	J. H. Whittlesey	194	May 18	Oct. 15	Oct. 19	6	16.0	**13.7**	14.4	19.8	**72.7**	Good cultivation.
Winnebago	Roscoe	A. J. Lovejoy	189	May 20	Oct. 13	Oct. 19	6	19.0	**13.1**	13.8	17.4	**78.9**	Good cultivation.
McHenry	Chemung	Joseph Kuhles	357	May 20	Nov. 1	Nov. 3	4	18.5	**15.1**	15.9	18.8	**84.3**	....
Carroll	Lanark	Jacob Grossman	373	May 10	Oct. 20	Nov. 3	6	16.5	**16.5**	17.4	20.9	**83.1**	Beets wilted. Injured by insects.
Carroll	Mt. Carroll	W. M. Keim	225	May 5	Oct. 18	Oct. 20	6	18.2	**14.4**	15.1	17.9	**84.4**	....
Carroll	Mt. Carroll	C. H. Keim	227	May 19	Oct. 18	Oct. 20	6	20.2	**12.1**	12.8	16.1	**79.3**	Good cultivation.
Carroll	Nursery	J. V. Cotta	124	May 13	Oct. 11	Oct. 14	6	24.2	**12.5**	13.2	16.7	**78.9**	Good cultivation.
Whiteside	Albany	G. H. Todd	271	Apr. 15	Oct. 22	Oct. 26	6	18.7	**12.5**	13.2	16.6	**79.5**	Poor cultivation.
Whiteside	Morrison	Simon Whistler	311	May 15	Oct. 23	Oct. 28	6	24.5	**14.3**	15.1	19.6	**77.1**	Poor cultivation.
Whiteside	Penrose	F. D. Myers	182	May 15	Oct. 14	Oct. 18	7	21.3	**14.2**	14.9	18.1	**82.4**	Good cultivation.
Whiteside	Penrose	F. D. Myers	272	......	Oct. 22	Oct. 26	4	32.0	**14.2**	15.0	18.2	**82.1**	Poor cultivation.
Whiteside	Penrose	F. D. Myers	273	......	Oct. 22	Oct. 26	4	35.3	**9.8**	10.3	13.7	**75.2**	Not Station seed.
Whiteside	Round Grove	C. W. Mitchell	154	May 12	Oct. 14	Oct. 16	6	16.0	**13.2**	13.9	17.4	**79.7**	....
Whiteside	Sterling	John Sanborn	396	......	Oct. 25	Nov. 12	5	19.6	**15.3**	16.1	21.5	**74.5**	Beets wilted.
Ogle	Byron	F. D. Linn	135	May 27	Oct. 12	Oct. 15	6	26.7	**14.9**	15.7	19.7	**79.6**	Good cultivation.
Ogle	Byron	W. F. Whitney	148	......	......	Oct. 15	5	22.0	**11.5**	12.1	17.4	**69.7**	....
Ogle	Polo	J. N. Sanborn	134	May 10	Oct. 11	Oct. 15	6	19.7	**11.4**	12.0	16.1	**74.5**	Surface cultivation.
Lee	Ashton	Aaron Albertson	97	May 16	Oct. 8	Oct. 13	6	12.0	**16.4**	17.3	22.3	**77.5**	....
Lee	Ashton	Ira R. George	151	May 10	Oct. 12	Oct. 16	6	17.2	**14.4**	15.1	18.3	**82.7**	Fair cultivation.
Lee	Dixon	J. C. Atkinson	345	May 1	Oct. 23	Oct. 30	6	14.8	**13.6**	14.3	17.6	**81.3**	Poor cultivation.
Lee	Dixon	J. L. McGinnis	234	......	......	Oct. 21	6	21.7	**8.8**	9.3	13.2	**70.1**	Two rows.
Lee	Dixon	Wm. McGinnis	224	May 15	Oct. 19	Oct. 20	9	6.0	**16.3**	17.2	20.1	**85.4**	Two rows.
Lee	Dixon	Aug. Schick	260	May 1	Oct. 19	Oct. 23	6	21.5	**12.6**	13.3	16.1	**82.6**	Fair cultivation.
Lee	Dixon	Frank Siefkin	192	May 20	Oct. 15	Oct. 19	6	21.0	**11.6**	12.2	16.0	**76.3**	Fair cultivation.
Lee	Dixon	N. L. Stary	374	May 18	Oct. 27	Nov. 3	6	9.8	**16.6**	17.5	19.7	**88.9**	Good cultivation.
DeKalb	Malta	Frank S. Corey	216	May 6	Oct. 16	Oct. 20	6	17.5	**16.3**	17.1	20.2	**84.7**	Good cultivation.
DeKalb	Malta	Frank S. Corey	356	May 6	Oct. 18	Nov. 3	6	20.3	**12.4**	13.0	17.2	**75.6**	Good cultivation.

DeKalb	Sycamore	P. M. Alden	261	May 26	Oct. 22	Oct. 25	6	26.0	**10.6**	11.2	15.1	**74.0**	Small plat.
DeKalb	Sycamore	John Gustafson	156	May 14	Oct. 13	Oct. 18	6	24.7	**15.2**	16.0	19.4	**82.7**	Good cultivation.
DeKalb	Sycamore	Edwin Waite	266	May 26	Oct. 23	Oct. 25	6	17.8	**10.6**	11.2	15.1	**73.8**	Not Station seed.
DeKalb	Sycamore	S. H. Willis	317	June 1	Oct. 15	Oct. 29	6	13.8	**15.7**	16.6	20.9	**79.1**	One row.
DeKalb	Sycamore	B. F. Wyman	263	May 15	Oct. 22	Oct. 25	6	22.0	**13.1**	13.8	17.6	**78.1**	Fair cultivation.
Dupage	Wayne	G. W. Pickering	74	May 31	Oct. 7	Oct. 11	6	20.8	**15.6**	16.4	20.0	**82.2**	Good cultivation.
Dupage	Wayne	G. W. Pickering	75	May 31	Oct. 7	Oct. 11	4	24.8	**11.1**	11.7	15.8	**74.3**	Not Station seed
Cook	Harvey	A. H. Gaston	64	Apr. 15	Oct. 7	Oct. 9	6	22.7	**14.1**	14.8	17.7	**83.4**	Thinning delayed.
Cook	Richton	Frank Stephens	295	May 20	Oct. 18	Oct. 27	2	33.5	**13.2**	13.9	17.3	**79.9**	....
Cook	Summit	D. Katt	259	May 13	Oct. 20	Oct. 23	5	16.6	**15.6**	16.4	19.3	**84.9**	Poor cultivation.
Rock Island	Illinois City	Theo Huber	232	... ...	Oct. 16	Oct. 21	6	16.0	**14.9**	15.7	19.0	**82.5**	Fair cultivation.
Henry	Galva	E. A. Cardiff	81	May 10	Oct. 9	Oct. 12	6	23.8	**11.6**	12.2	15.4	**79.1**	Fair cultivation.
Henry	Galva	Lloyd Z. Jones	195	May 28	Oct. 15	Oct. 19	6	17.7	**13.0**	13.7	17.1	**79.8**	Good cultivation.
Henry	Geneseo	E. W. Deming	308	June 1	Oct. 26	Oct. 28	6	13.2	**11.3**	11.9	16.5	**72.0**	Good cultivation.
Henry	Hooppole	John Minch	347	June 11	Oct. 29	Nov. 2	6	21.7	**14.6**	15.4	19.1	**80.2**	Fair cultivation.
Henry	Pink Prairie	Geo. Riley	125	Apr. 2	Oct. 8	Oct. 14	6	17.3	**13.4**	14.1	17.0	**82.5**	Fair cultivation.
Henry	Souders	Frank Perkins	313	May 28	Oct. 23	Oct. 28	6	11.5	**12.4**	13.0	17.1	**76.3**	Good cultivation.
Bureau	Lamoille	Chas. Schnuckle	41	May 11	Sept. 27	Sept. 30	5	55.4	**10.0**	10.6	14.3	**74.0**	Leaves injured.
Bureau	Princeton	Clem. Freeman	217	May 7	Oct. 18	Oct. 20	6	21.7	**11.6**	12.2	15.5	**78.8**	Good cultivation.
Bureau	Walnut	T. F. Stroud	235	May 8	Oct. 15	Oct. 21	6	20.7	**9.8**	10.4	13.5	**76.7**	....
Lasalle	Deer Park	F. H. Tiffany	68	May 2	Oct. 7	Oct. 9	6	20.7	**12.9**	13.6	16.4	**82.7**	Very little attention.
Lasalle	Marseilles	A. C. Galloway	77	May 15	Oct. 9	Oct. 11	6	13.7	**13.0**	13.7	16.9	**81.0**	One cultivation.
Lasalle	Mendota	E. W. Shearburn	372	May 27	Oct. 28	Nov. 3	6	17.8	**11.0**	11.6	16.0	**72.2**	Good cultivation.
Lasalle	Mendota	Wm. Truman	157	May 20	Oct. 14	Oct. 18	6	24.8	**13.0**	13.7	17.1	**80.1**	Beets wilted.
Lasalle	Ottawa	Frank L. Beach	226	May 10	Oct. 15	Oct. 20	4	18.8	**12.0**	12.6	16.7	**75.5**	Good cultivation.
Lasalle	Ottawa	Jno. H. Center	205	June 20	Oct. 11	Oct. 19	6	16.0	**9.8**	10.4	14.6	**70.8**	One row.
Lasalle	Ottawa	J. N. Dunaway	76	May 25	Oct. 8	Oct. 11	6	16.8	**10.8**	11.4	15.5	**73.8**	Raised in garden.
Lasalle	Ottawa	J. N. Dunaway	380	....	....	Nov. 5	5	12.6	**13.8**	14.5	18.4	**78.8**	....
Lasalle	Ottawa	Fiske & Beem	279	....	....	Oct. 26	4	17.5	**14.5**	15.3	18.0	**84.9**	....
Lasalle	Ottawa	Fiske & Beem	377	....	....	Nov. 5	6	20.2	**14.7**	15.5	19.0	**81.2**	....
Lasalle	Ottawa	Fiske & Beem	402	....	....	Nov. 16	4	14.5	**11.5**	12.1	15.2	**79.9**	....
Lasalle	Ottawa	James Ford	184	May 15	Oct. 14	Oct. 19	6	27.3	**15.5**	16.3	20.0	**81.4**	Poor cultivation.
Lasalle	Ottawa	Lorenzo Leland	60	....	....	Oct. 9	7	31.0	**13.1**	13.8	17.1	**80.2**	....
Lasalle	Ottawa	Lorenzo Leland	185	....	....	Oct. 19	7	18.6	**13.2**	13.9	17.2	**80.7**	....
Lasalle	Ottawa	Lorenzo Leland	352	....	....	Nov. 2	6	19.5	**15.0**	15.8	19.1	**82.3**	Fair cultivation.
Lasalle	Ottawa	I. B. Lovejoy	207	May 12	Oct. 13	Oct. 19	6	19.7	**14.3**	15.1	17.7	**85.0**	Fair cultivation.
Lasalle	Ottawa	I. B. Lovejoy	400	May 10	Nov. 11	Nov. 16	6	16.0	**14.4**	15.2	18.6	**81.8**	Fair cultivation.

TABLE 1.—CONTINUED.

County.	Town.	Grower.	Lab. No.	Planted.	Harvested.	Analyzed.	No. analyzed	Average weight, oz.	Per cent. Sugar in beets.	Per cent. Sugar in juice.	Per cent. Solids in juice.	Purity coefficient.	Remarks.
Lasalle......	Ottawa........	Frank Porcheur	84	Apr. 25	Oct. 8	Oct. 12	6	31.5	**12.5**	13.2	15.4	**85.3**	....
Lasalle......	Ottawa........	W. E. Pritchard	208	......	......	Oct. 19	6	30.2	**12.5**	13.2	16.5	**80.0**	....
Lasalle......	Ottawa........	W. E. Pritchard	209	......	......	Oct. 19	6	28.0	**13.2**	13.9	17 2	**80.5**	....
Lasalle......	Ottawa........	W. E. Pritchard	378	......	......	Nov. 5	6	19.2	**15.1**	15.9	19.0	**83.7**	....
Lasalle......	Ottawa........	W. E. Pritchard	379	......	......	Nov. 5	6	25.7	**14.5**	15.3	18.7	**81.8**	....
Lasalle......	Ottawa........	Andrew Rorem.	267	May 15	Oct. 22	Oct. 26	6	15.3	**11.6**	12.2	16.0	**76.4**	Fair cultivation.
Lasalle......	Ottawa........	E. H. Strait....	280	......	......	Oct. 26	6	16.5	**9.9**	10.4	14.6	**71.1**	One row.
Lasalle......	Ottawa........	Gibson Strawn..	371	......	Oct. 15	Nov. 3	6	20.2	**16.5**	17.4	20.4	**85.3**	Beets wilted.
Lasalle......	Ottawa........	Frank Trumbo..	204	May 15	Oct. 15	Oct. 19	6	25.5	**10.7**	11.3	15.3	**73.8**	....
Lasalle......	Ottawa........	M. P. Trumbo..	206	......	Oct. 15	Oct. 19	6	49.2	**11.3**	11.9	15.2	**78.3**	Poor cultivation.
Lasalle......	Ottawa........	M. P. Trumbo..	355	May 15	Oct. 27	Nov. 3	6	24.2	**13.1**	13.8	17.3	**79.5**	Two rows.
Lasalle......	Ottawa........	Edw. J. Vernon.	278	May 25	Oct. 18	Oct. 26	5	12.6	**14.3**	15.1	18.0	**84.1**	Good cultivation.
Lasalle......	Prairie Center..	L. E Sampson..	316	May 21	Oct. 24	Oct. 29	6	18.3	**16.3**	17.2	19.6	**87.8**	Fair cultivation.
Lasalle......	Utica..........	J. J. Aubry.....	215	May 10	Oct. 17	Oct. 20	6	24.5	**12.6**	13.3	16.8	**79.3**	Fair cultivation.
Kendall.....	Bristol........	G. G. Hunt....	236	May 15	Oct. 9	Oct. 21	6	10.8	**14.4**	15.2	18.0	**84.4**	Beets wilted.
Kendall.....	Newark.......	A. Vanriper....	375	June 1	Oct. 15	Nov. 5	6	17.3	**13.2**	13.9	17.1	**81.2**	Good cultivation.
Grundy......	Morris........	G. W. Ridings..	190	May 15	Oct. 15	Oct. 19	6	18.2	**13 9**	14.6	18.2	**80.2**	Good cultivation.
Will........	Bemes........	Chas. Batterman	292	May 20	Oct. 20	Oct. 27	2	66.0	**12.2**	12.8	16.2	**78.9**	....
Will........	Bemes........	Fred Seehansen	300	May 19	Oct. 20	Oct. 27	3	13.0	**15.1**	15.9	18.4	**86.0**	....
Will........	Crete	Chas. Bissett...	296	May 17	Oct. 18	Oct. 27	3	25.7	**10.0**	10.5	13.4	**78.2**	....
Will........	Crete.........	D. T. Bordwell.	281	May 19	Oct. 19	Oct. 27	3	24.0	**11.8**	12.5	17.1	**72.9**	Good cultivation.
Will........	Crete.........	J. W. Dierson..	298	May 16	Oct. 21	Oct. 27	3	18.7	**15.2**	16.0	19.0	**83.8**	....
Will........	Crete.........	Wm. H. Dierson	299	May 16	Oct. 20	Oct. 27	3	21.0	**12.9**	13.6	17.0	**79.9**	....
Will........	Crete.........	John Dodge	306	May 8	Oct. 18	Oct. 27	3	27.7	**13.6**	14.3	18.7	**76.5**	....
Will........	Crete.........	Henry Drunsing	282	May 19	Oct. 20	Oct. 27	3	17.7	**15.3**	16.1	18.8	**85.5**	....
Will........	Crete.........	Louis Grote....	286	May 20	Oct. 18	Oct. 27	2	26.5	**15.1**	15.9	19.0	**83.3**	....
Will........	Crete.........	Conrad Halle...	285	May 15	Oct. 18	Oct. 27	2	26.0	**14.4**	15.2	18.4	**82.3**	....
Will........	Crete.........	Chas. Klemme..	294	May 10	Oct. 18	Oct. 27	3	19.3	**11.6**	12.2	15.0	**80.8**	....

Will	Crete	H. Kracke	301	May 8	Oct. 20	Oct. 27	2	33.0	**10.6**	11.2	15.0	**74.2**	
Will	Crete	R. B. Millar	302	May 20	Oct. 12	Oct. 27	6	17.0	**12.2**	12.8	17.6	**72.6**	Injured by bugs.
Will	Crete	Fred Wilkening	290	May 10	Oct. 18	Oct. 27	3	26.7	**13.3**	14.0	17.6	**79.5**	
Will	Goodenow	Harry Fluck	303	May 19	Oct. 20	Oct. 27	3	25.3	**13.8**	14.6	17.9	**81.2**	
Will	Goodenow	Alex. Jackson	307	May 12	Oct. 19	Oct. 27	3	31.3	**10.0**	10.5	14.1	**74.4**	Not Station seed.
Will	Joliet	O. W. Laraway	348	May 15	Oct. 25	Nov. 2	6	18.0	**14.9**	15.7	19.3	**80.9**	Fair cultivation.
Will	Peotone	G. N. Barton	291	May 20	Oct. 19	Oct. 27	3	40.3	**11.0**	11.6	15.4	**75.2**	
Will	Peotone	Moses Bowe	293	May 7	Oct. 19	Oct. 27	2	49.0	**13.2**	13.9	18.1	**76.6**	
Will	Peotone	John Cann	283	May 20	Oct. 19	Oct. 27	2	46.5	**10.9**	11.5	15.0	**76.2**	
Will	Peotone	A. P. Lilly	287	May 7	Oct. 19	Oct. 27	3	21.0	**9.9**	10.5	14.9	**70.4**	
Will	Peotone	Chas. Peck	288	May 7	Oct. 19	Oct. 27	2	35.0	**15.6**	16.5	19.6	**83.8**	
Will	Wilmington	Thos. Lacey	255	May 20	Oct. 21	Oct. 22	6	21.8	**14.3**	15.1	18.1	**83.0**	Fair cultivation.
Kankakee	Essex	A. Gregson	43	May 10	Oct. 6	Oct. 8	6	19.7	**12.6**	13.3	17.2	**77.2**	Good cultivation.
Kankakee	Grant Park	Jno. B. Hayhurst	297	May 23	Oct. 21	Oct. 27	2	48.0	**10.5**	11.0	14.1	**77.9**	
Kankakee	Grant Park	O. C. Parmalee	305	May 7	Oct. 21	Oct. 27	3	22.7	**12.4**	13.1	16.2	**80.7**	One row.
Kankakee	Hopkins Park	T. Glinstra	187	May 12	Oct. 14	Oct. 19	6	19.2	**11.6**	12.3	15.9	**77.0**	
Kankakee	Kankakee	E. D. Nichols	188	May 24	Oct. 11	Oct. 19	6	20.7	**14.4**	15.1	20.2	**74.7**	Good cultivation.
Kankakee	Kankakee	Jas. R. Smiley	397	May 24	Nov. 7	Nov. 12	6	19.2	**14.5**	15.3	18.5	**82.6**	Good cultivation.
Kankakee	Waldron	J. E. Barlow	46	May 20	Sept. 27	Oct. 8	6	27.2	**13.7**	14.5	17.8	**81.4**	Beets wilted. Injured by bugs.
Kankakee	Waldron	B. W. Benedict	45	May 22	Oct. 5	Oct. 8	6	13.2	**14.0**	14.7	17.7	**83.2**	

One hundred and forty-three samples from thirty counties of Central Illinois.

[Do not include samples from Station farm.]

Mercer	Hamlet	C. A. Bopes	398	May 22	Nov. 4	Nov. 12	6	17.0	**12.6**	13.3	16.6	**79.7**	Fair cultivation.
Henderson	Stronghurst	Oscar W. Beckett	80	May 15	Oct. 9	Oct. 12	6	22.2	**9.2**	9.7	13.6	**70.8**	Injured by bugs.
Knox	Abingdon	Jno. W. Head	78	May 10	Oct. 9	Oct. 11	6	20.7	**9.7**	10.3	13.8	**74.3**	Fair cultivation.
Knox	Galesburg	A. C. Higgins	408	May 20	Nov. ..	Nov. 23	3	20.0	**12.6**	13.3	16.8	**78.7**	
Knox	Galesburg	C. A. Hinckley	407	May 20	Nov. 13	Nov. 23	6	15.3	**11.6**	12.3	16.0	**76.7**	Garden cultivation.
Knox	Williamsfield	W. S. Baird	42	May 10	Sept. 28	Oct. 1	5	23.4	**10.3**	10.9	15.4	**70.7**	
Stark	Wyoming	W. P. Turner	150	Apr. 15	Oct. 13	Oct. 16	6	10.3	**14.4**	15.2	19.4	**78.3**	Tops eaten by rabbits.
Peoria	Dunlap	I. B. Yates	122	May 27	Oct. 7	Oct. 14	6	20.3	**11.5**	12.2	15.8	**76.8**	Poor stand.
Peoria	Mossville	Adam Bauer	130	May ..	Oct. 1	Oct. 14	6	10.5	**17.4**	18.4	21.7	**84.8**	Beets much wilted.
Peoria	Northampton	R. W. Gilliam	83	May 10	Oct. 10	Oct. 12	6	28.2	**11.2**	11.8	14.9	**79.0**	One row.
Peoria	Trivoli	P. A. Arnold	95	May 26	Oct. 11	Oct. 13	6	36.0	**11.9**	12.5	15.7	**79.9**	Fair cultivation.
Marshall	Lawn Ridge	N. E. Nurss	128	May 29	Oct. 11	Oct. 14	6	18.3	**14.3**	15.1	17.9	**83.9**	Fair cultivation.
Woodford	Eureka	C. C. Price	221	May 7	Oct. 19	Oct. 20	6	22.3	**13.3**	14.0	17.0	**82.1**	Good cultivation.
Livingston	Odell	Wm. L. Walker	90	May 10	Oct. 9	Oct. 13	6	20.3	**14.2**	15.0	18.1	**82.8**	Poor cultivation.

TABLE 1.—CONTINUED.

County.	Town.	Grower.	Lab. No.	Planted.	Harvested.	Analyzed.	No. analyzed	Average weight, oz.	Per cent. Sugar in beets.	Per cent. Sugar in juice.	Per cent. Solids in juice.	Purity coefficient.	Remarks.
Livingston ..	Pontiac	F. L. Paddleford	393	Apr. 28	Oct. 27	Nov. 9	6	16.0	**14.8**	15.6	17.9	**87.0**	Fair cultivation.
Livingston ..	Strawn	W. P. Goembel.	65	May 15	Oct. 7	Oct. 9	6	14.7	**13.0**	13.7	17.3	**79.0**	Little cultivation.
Iroquois	Danforth.	Al. Brumback..	71	May 14	Oct. 8	Oct. 11	6	23.2	**13.8**	14.5	17.7	**82.1**	Fair cultivation.
Iroquois	Gilman	F. I. Mann....	197	May 25	Oct. 12	Oct. 19	6	22.3	**13.6**	14.3	17.7	**80.8**	Fair cultivation.
Iroquois ...	Loda	R. O. Hollister..	62	May 5	Oct. 7	Oct. 9	6	24.0	**13.2**	13.9	17.1	**81.1**	Ground mulched.
Iroquois	Onarga	E. J. Baker	57	June 1	Oct. 6	Oct. 8	5	24.0	**9.8**	10.4	14.8	**70.1**	Two rows.
Iroquois	Onarga	J. B. Boyer ..	98	May 10	Oct. 8	Oct. 13	5	16.0	**10.8**	11.4	15.9	**71.9**	Two rows.
Iroquois ...	Onarga	J. B. Boyer	103	June 1	Oct. 8	Oct. 13	5	8.6	**13.9**	14.7	19.4	**75.7**	Two rows.
Iroquois ...	Onarga	R. B. Cultra ...	169	May 20	Oct. 9	Oct. 18	5	20.4	**11.3**	11.9	16.1	**73.8**	One row.
Iroquois	Onarga	Chas. David....	112	May 15	Oct. 7	Oct. 13	5	11.4	**11.6**	12.2	16.7	**73.0**	Two rows.
Iroquois	Onarga	W. A. Davis....	116	June 1	Oct. 7	Oct. 13	5	14.2	**11.6**	12.3	17.5	**69.9**	One row.
Iroquois	Onarga	W. A. Davis....	117	May 10	Oct. 7	Oct. 13	5	12.6	**10.2**	10.8	15.6	**68.8**	One row.
Iroquois	Onarga	S. F. Everett ..	165	May 20	Oct. 11	Oct. 18	5	14.4	**11.1**	11.7	15.9	**73.6**	One row.
Iroquois	Onarga	Jacob Farr.....	107	May 25	Oct. 7	Oct. 13	5	17.2	**13.0**	13.7	17.0	**80.1**	Two rows.
Iroquois	Onarga	C. O. Frantz ...	114	May 10	Oct. 7	Oct. 13	5	19.6	**9.9**	10.4	14.1	**73.7**	One row.
Iroquois ...	Onarga	C. O. Frantz ...	118	May 20	Oct. 7	Oct. 13	5	15.2	**7.3**	7.7	11.6	**65.8**	One row.
Iroquois	Onarga	Geo. Gleason...	106	May 15	Oct. 7	Oct. 13	5	24.6	**10.9**	11.5	14.9	**77.1**	One row.
Iroquois	Onarga	E. Gould	176	May 7	Oct. 14	Oct. 18	5	15.8	**11.1**	11.7	15.3	**76.3**	One row.
Iroquois ..	Onarga	G. E. Hagerman	108	May 20	Oct. 8	Oct. 13	5	17.8	**12.5**	13.1	16.6	**78.8**	Two rows.
Iroquois	Onarga	C. Hartshorn...	168	May 10	Oct. 11	Oct. 18	5	17.6	**10.8**	11.4	14.4	**79.2**	One row.
Iroquois	Onarga	Reuben Havens	111	May 15	Oct. 7	Oct. 13	5	23.2	**10.6**	11.2	15.4	**72.3**	One row.
Iroquois	Onarga	H. F. Hollister.	174	May 25	Oct. 14	Oct. 18	5	14.4	**12.5**	13.2	17.1	**77.0**	One row.
Iroquois	Onarga	J. Inskip..	56	May 15	Oct. 6	Oct. 8	5	21.4	**9.9**	10.4	13.5	**77.2**	One row.
Iroquois	Onarga	J. H. Jarvis....	175	May 15	Oct. 14	Oct. 18	5	11.6	**12.6**	13.3	16.9	**78.6**	One row.
Iroquois ...	Onarga	H. Knoche.....	177	May 15	Oct. 14	Oct. 18	5	15.0	**9.6**	10.1	14.4	**69.7**	One row.
Iroquois	Onarga	E. G. Latham..	170	May 20	Oct. 11	Oct. 18	5	15.2	**13.5**	14.2	17.5	**81.1**	One row.
Iroquois	Onarga	S. W. Laughlin.	55	May 25	Oct. 6	Oct. 8	5	25.4	**12.7**	13.4	16.3	**82.1**	One row.
Iroquois	Onarga	J. B. Lawson...	167	May 10	Oct. 11	Oct. 18	5	19.6	**12.3**	13.0	16.7	**77.5**	One row.

Iroquois	Onarga	J. B. Lawson	172	May 25	Oct. 11	Oct. 11	5	19.6	**12.9**	13.6	16.7	**81.1**	One row.
Iroquois	Onarga	Rob't Looker	173	May 25	Oct. 9	Oct. 18	5	15.8	**9.0**	9.5	12.8	**73.8**	Two rows.
Iroquois	Onarga	Hiram Lowe	113	June 8	Oct. 7	Oct. 13	5	25.2	**10.9**	11.5	14.7	**77.8**	One row.
Iroquois	Onarga	Samuel Major	104	May 15	Oct. 8	Oct. 13	5	15.0	**10.4**	10.9	15.6	**70.1**	Two rows.
Iroquois	Onarga	D. Martin	102	May 25	Oct. 8	Oct. 13	5	21.8	**11.4**	12.0	16.2	**74.3**	One row.
Iroquois	Onarga	Rob't Meredith	105	May 20	Oct. 8	Oct. 13	5	21.4	**10.7**	11.3	15.0	**74.8**	One row.
Iroquois	Onarga	S. R. Nickerson	110	May 30	Oct. 7	Oct. 13	5	22.4	**11.5**	12.1	16.2	**74.6**	One row.
Iroquois	Onarga	Dan Parmalee	115	May 25	Oct. 6	Oct. 13	5	23.8	**10.0**	10.5	14.1	**74.3**	One row.
Iroquois	Onarga	John Pearson	164	May 5	Oct. 11	Oct. 18	5	21.4	**13.3**	14.0	17.2	**81.2**	Good cultivation.
Iroquois	Onarga	Job Pearson	166	May 15	Oct. 11	Oct. 18	5	17.6	**11.2**	11.8	14.9	**78.9**	One row.
Iroquois	Onarga	J. W. Porter	178	May 15	Oct. 14	Oct. 18	5	19.4	**12.9**	13.6	16.6	**81.9**	One row.
Iroquois	Onarga	Geo. Sinderson	52	May 15	Oct. 6	Oct. 8	5	28.0	**9.8**	10.3	13.9	**74.3**	One row.
Iroquois	Onarga	Miss E. Slinn	51	May 15	Oct. 6	Oct. 8	5	35.8	**9.1**	9.6	13.4	**71.4**	One row.
Iroquois	Onarga	R. N. Spellman	180	May 10	Oct. 14	Oct. 18	5	17.6	**9.6**	10.1	14.7	**68.4**	Poor cultivation.
Iroquois	Onarga	L. T. Stoutemyer	109	June 1	Oct. 7	Oct. 13	5	24.8	**12.1**	12.7	16.4	**77.3**	Two rows.
Iroquois	Onarga	Dan'l Strevy	100	May 25	Oct. 8	Oct. 13	5	19.2	**11.0**	11.6	16.4	**70.6**	One row.
Iroquois	Onarga	Ben Theesfelt	101	May 25	Oct. 8	Oct. 13	5	15.2	**11.6**	12.3	17.5	**70.2**	Two rows.
Iroquois	Onarga	Chas. Theesfelt	99	May 30	Oct. 8	Oct. 13	5	21.0	**12.8**	13.5	17.5	**77.1**	Two rows.
Iroquois	Onarga	G. A. Weagant	58	May 10	Oct. 6	Oct. 8	5	20.2	**10.3**	10.9	15.0	**72.5**	Two rows.
Iroquois	Onarga	S. A. Whiteside	179	May 15	Oct. 14	Oct 18	5	20.0	**12.2**	12.9	16.8	**76.5**	Poor cultivation.
Iroquois	Onarga	Isaac Whitted	47	May 30	Oct. 6	Oct. 8	5	51.0	**8.1**	8.6	12.2	**70.3**	One row.
Iroquois	Onarga	Isaac Wilson	171	May 15	Oct. 11	Oct. 18	5	18.4	**10.1**	10.6	14.7	**71.9**	One row.
Iroquois	Ridgeville	D. T. Hamer	181	May 15	Oct. 14	Oct. 18	5	13.8	**14.2**	15.0	18.7	**80.0**	One row.
Iroquois	Sheldon	Henry Dillon	193	May 17	Oct. 15	Oct. 19	5	19.4	**14.1**	14.8	19.2	**77.0**	Fair cultivation.
Hancock	Sonora	C. P. Golden	196	May 12	Oct. 12	Oct. 19	6	17.3	**10.6**	11.2	17.5	**64.0**	One row.
Fulton	Leeseburg	E. H. Diehl	354	May 25	Oct. 29	Nov. 2	6	16.5	**11.2**	11.8	15.2	**77.1**	Poor cultivation.
Tazewell	Delavan	Ralph Allen	351	May 1	Oct. 14	Nov. 2	6	18.2	**15.2**	16.0	19.1	**83.6**	Beets wilted.
Tazewell	Morton	W. H. Conibear	121	May 15	Oct. 11	Oct. 14	6	21.5	**9.5**	10.0	13.5	**74.1**	Good cultivation.
McLean	Bloomington	W. H. Foster	63	May 19	Oct. 7	Oct. 9	6	22.5	**15.0**	15.8	18.6	**84.5**	Good cultivation.
McLean	Bloomington	Jno. F. Rhodes	269	May 1	Oct. 22	Oct. 26	6	25.0	**12.6**	13.3	17.4	**76.6**	Fair cultivation.
McLean	Ellsworth	Frank Virgiel	44	May 11	Oct. 7	Oct. 8	6	29.2	**10.5**	11.0	14.9	**74.0**	Fair cultivation.
McLean	Leroy	G. W. Hedrick	82	May 4	Oct. 8	Oct. 12	6	22.0	**9.2**	9.7	12.9	**74.6**	....
McLean	Padua	M. L. Wightman	314	May 5	Oct. 11	Oct. 28	6	19.3	**12.8**	13.5	17.2	**78.4**	Poor cultivation.
Ford	Gibson City	J. B. Wallace	61	May 6	Oct. 6	Oct. 9	6	24.3	**10.8**	11.4	14.7	**77.0**	....
Adams	Camp Point	L. G. Hoke	132	May 20	Oct. 11	Oct. 15	6	20.7	**11.4**	12.0	16.5	**72.6**	Injured by bugs.
Adams	Camp Point	L. G. Hoke	133	May 20	Oct. 11	Oct. 15	6	9.5	**16.4**	17.3	21.2	**81.5**	Injured by bugs.
Adams	Payson	D. E. Robbins	159	Apr. 27	Oct. 13	Oct. 18	6	18.0	**12.1**	12.8	16.9	**75.6**	Beets wilted.

TABLE 1.—CONTINUED.

County.	Town.	Grower.	Lab. No.	Planted.	Harvested.	Analyzed.	No. analyzed	Average weight, oz.	Per cent. Sugar in beets.	Per cent. Sugar in juice.	Per cent. Solids in juice.	Purity coefficient.	Remarks.
Adams	Quincy	Herbert Turner	219	May 15	Oct. 13	Oct. 20	6	18.0	**9.8**	10.3	14.2	**72.6**	Good cultivation.
Mason	Bath	Frank Markert	200	May 23	Oct. 16	Oct. 19	6	18.2	**14.3**	15.0	18.4	**81.5**	Good cultivation.
Mason	Easton	C. L. Buchanan	239	Apr. 20	Oct. 13	Oct. 21	6	20.2	**9.9**	10.4	14.4	**72.1**	Beets wilted.
Mason	Easton	Mark Cooper	238	May 15	Oct. 13	Oct. 21	6	30.8	**8.6**	9.1	13.2	**69.0**	Beets wilted.
Mason	Easton	Geo. Helbert	240	June 20	Oct. 15	Oct. 21	6	33.3	**9.2**	9.7	13.9	**69.7**	Beets wilted.
Mason	Easton	R. B. Samuell	92	May 15	Oct. 11	Oct. 13	6	16.3	**9.1**	9.6	14.4	**66.6**	Not fair test.
Mason	Easton	Henry Unkin	241	May 10	Oct. 2	Oct. 21	4	44.5	**8.4**	8.8	13.2	**66.7**	Beets much wilted.
Mason	Forest City	Geo. E. Barnes	136	May 10	Oct. 11	Oct. 15	5	32.6	**9.6**	10.1	13.1	**77.3**	Fair cultivation.
Mason	Forest City	W. R. Barnes	142	May 1	Oct. 9	Oct. 15	6	18.3	**10.3**	10.9	15.3	**71.1**	Fair cultivation.
Mason	Forest City	A. D. Bowser	137	May 20	Oct. 11	Oct. 15	6	20.0	**9.8**	10.4	15.3	**67.8**	....
Mason	Forest City	A. D. Bowser	139	May 20	Oct. 11	Oct. 15	6	19.0	**9.9**	10.4	16.0	**65.1**	Fair cultivation.
Mason	Forest City	W. S. Coryell	144	May ..	Oct. 11	Oct. 15	6	9.5	**12.9**	13.6	18.5	**73.4**	Poor cultivation.
Mason	Forest City	J. R. Gillmore	141	Apr. 27	Oct. 11	Oct. 15	6	20.8	**9.1**	9.6	13.3	**72.0**	....
Mason	Forest City	Frank Lewis	131	May 25	Oct. 11	Oct. 15	6	6.2	**14.3**	15.0	19.4	**77.5**	Good cultivation.
Mason	Forest City	G. W. Neikirk	146	May 15	Oct. 11	Oct. 15	6	8.7	**14.1**	14.9	18.5	**80.4**	Poor cultivation.
Mason	Forest City	L. N. Neikirk	138	June 1	Oct. 11	Oct. 15	6	25.3	**13.7**	14.5	17.7	**81.9**	Fair cultivation.
Mason	Forest City	F. G. Onstatt	140	May 20	Oct. 11	Oct. 15	6	8.0	**12.8**	13.5	17.1	**79.2**	Fair cultivation.
Mason	Forest City	John Rabe	145	May 15	Oct. 9	Oct. 15	6	12.8	**13.3**	14.0	17.6	**79.6**	Fair cultivation.
Mason	Forest City	G. W. Scott	143	May 3	Oct. 3	Oct. 15	6	10.5	**14.7**	15.5	20.7	**75.0**	Beets wilted.
Mason	Havana	H. Borgelt, sr.	201	......	Oct. 16	Oct. 19	6	10.3	**9.7**	10.2	14.3	**71.3**	....
Mason	Havana	A. H. Dierker	202	May 25	Oct. 15	Oct. 19	6	12.5	**12.7**	13.4	16.4	**81.6**	One row.
Mason	Havana	G. Dierker	199	......	......	Oct. 19	6	15.7	**9.7**	10.3	14.6	**70.2**	....
Mason	Havana	H. Dierker	203	May 30	Oct. 15	Oct. 19	6	19.8	**9.4**	9.9	13.3	**74.3**	One row.
Mason	Havana	Henry Hahn	213	May 3	Oct. 18	Oct. 20	6	16.0	**10.2**	10.7	15.2	**70.5**	....
Mason	Havana	G. G. Hopping	222	Apr. 30	Oct. 18	Oct. 20	6	21.7	**14.5**	15.3	19.9	**77.0**	With strawberries.
Mason	Manito	H. S. Latham	315	May 10	Oct. 26	Oct. 28	6	12.5	**7.4**	7.8	10.7	**72.6**	Good cultivation.
Logan	Lincoln	R. W. Braucher	384	May 1	Nov. 1	Nov. 6	6	17.5	**11.3**	11.9	15.1	**79.1**	Good cultivation.
Logan	Lincoln	Mrs. Hummels	381	......	Oct. 20	Nov. 5	3	16.3	**9.7**	10.2	15.8	**64.2**	Beets wilted.

Logan	Lincoln	Sam Logan	383	......	Oct. 30	Nov. 5	4	57.3	**11.0**	11.6	15.8	**73.4**	Fair cultivation.
Logan	Lincoln	J. Wilson	382	......	Oct. 22	Nov. 5	3	23.3	**7.2**	7.6	12.3	**61.8**	....
Dewitt	Weldon	S. W. Baker	73	May 8	Oct. 8	Oct. 11	6	27.0	**13.8**	14.5	17.8	**81.7**	Good cultivation.
Macon	Decatur	W. T. Walmsley	349	Apr. 29	Oct. 23	Nov. 2	6	18.2	**8.0**	8.4	12.9	**64.9**	Good cultivation.
Piatt	Bement	G. L. & C. M. Burgess	318	June 1	Oct. 24	Oct. 29	6	20.5	**13.2**	13.9	17.3	**80.3**	Fair cultivation.
Piatt	Bement	A. S. Burr	310	May 25	Oct. 26	Oct. 28	6	19.5	**12.5**	13.2	16.1	**81.8**	One row.
Champaign	Ivesdale	B. B. Wirwatz	401	......	......	Nov. 16	6	23.0	**12.1**	12.7	16.7	**76.2**	....
Champaign	Rising	E. E. McKee	160	May 8	Oct. 15	Oct. 18	6	18.2	**13.8**	14.5	17.5	**83.0**	Beets wilted.
Champaign	Sidney	I. S. Raymond	262	......	Oct. 22	Oct. 25	6	12.7	**13.0**	13.7	16.2	**84.8**	Fair cultivation.
Champaign	Thomasboro	Henry Susdorf	59	Apr. 28	Oct. 7	Oct. 9	5	18.4	**12.0**	12.7	16.1	**78.4**	....
Champaign	Urbana	J. L. Dewey	394	May 1	Nov. 9	Nov. 9	6	20.2	**8.8**	9.3	13.7	**67.5**	....
Champaign	Urbana	J. L. Kerr	152	May 20	Oct. 13	Oct. 16	6	16.2	**12.5**	13.2	16.7	**78.9**	Fair cultivation.
Champaign	Urbana	J. L. Kerr	399	May 20	Nov. 15	Nov. 16	6	24.5	**12.5**	13.2	16.5	**80.0**	....
Champaign	Urbana	Nelson Reid	69	Apr. 28	Oct. 9	Oct. 9	4	29.3	**11.2**	11.8	14.1	**83.2**	Fair cultivation.
Champaign	Urbana	Nelson Reid	70	Apr. 24	Oct. 9	Oct. 9	3	30.3	**9.7**	10.2	13.3	**76.6**	Fair cultivation.
Champaign	Urbana	Nelson Reid	229	Apr. 28	Oct. 20	Oct. 20	6	19.8	**11.8**	12.4	14.1	**87.9**	....
Vermilion	Catlin	Sy Sandusky	186	May 23	Oct. 12	Oct. 19	6	20.8	**12.2**	12.9	16.2	**79.2**	Fair cultivation.
Vermilion	Indianola	Ira Kelsheimer	161	Apr. 28	Oct. 13	Oct. 18	6	16.2	**10.4**	11.0	15.4	**71.2**	Beets wilted.
Pike	Griggsville	R. P. Allen	162	May 1	Oct. 13	Oct. 18	4	10.0	**9.6**	10.1	14.5	**69.4**	Injured by bugs.
Scott	Manchester	John C. Andros	376	June 2	Oct. 20	Nov. 5	6	10.2	**9.7**	10.3	15.9	**64.3**	Beets wilted.
Morgan	Bethel	H. Bosse	274	May 15	Oct. 9	Oct. 26	6	22.8	**11.2**	11.8	15.0	**78.4**	Beets wilted.
Morgan	Bethel	L. H. Callaway	276	May 15	Oct. 11	Oct. 26	6	21.2	**11.6**	12.3	15.6	**78.5**	One row.
Morgan	Chapin	J. H. Ommen	275	May 10	Oct. 11	Oct. 26	6	21.3	**9.4**	9.9	13.9	**71.3**	Beets wilted.
Morgan	Concord	C. D. Baylus	277	May 31	Oct. 18	Oct. 26	6	24.2	**9.1**	9.6	13.8	**69.2**	Good cultivation.
Sangamon	Springfield	Chas. R. Price	120	May 20	Oct. 11	Oct. 14	6	17.0	**11.1**	11.7	14.8	**78.6**	....
Sangamon	Williamsville	Geo. E Lake	149	May 25	Oct. 13	Oct. 16	6	17.3	**11.3**	11.9	15.8	**75.1**	One row.
Christian	Morrisonville	Frank Grundy	91	May 17	Oct. 11	Oct. 13	6	16.3	**12.9**	13.6	17.6	**77.1**	Fair cultivation
Christian	Stonington	T. J. Bauer	96	June 10	Oct. 9	Oct. 13	6	21.8	**10.8**	11.4	15.0	**75.9**	Injured by chipmunks.
Shelby	Moweaqua	Rob't B. Wilson	127	Apr. 15	Oct. 12	Oct. 14	6	15.2	**13.3**	14.0	18.1	**77.2**	Fair cultivation.
Shelby	Moweaqua	Rob't B. Wilson	237	Apr. 12	Oct. 19	Oct. 21	6	16.3	**10.0**	10.6	15.4	**68.6**	One row.
Shelby	Shelbyville	Fred Zeigler	155	May 10	Oct. 10	Oct. 18	6	31.0	**9.6**	10.1	14.5	**69.9**	Beets wilted.
Douglas	Arcola	Jos. Combe	350	May 20	Oct. 28	Nov. 2	5	18.5	**10.5**	11.1	14.6	**75.5**	Fair cultivation.
Douglas	Hindsboro	C. A. Curtis	79	Apr. 15	Oct. 8	Oct. 11	5	30.8	**10.3**	10.8	14.1	**76.8**	....
Douglas	Newman	J. F. Stout	126	May 22	Oct. 11	Oct. 14	6	21.7	**12.8**	13.5	16.8	**80.2**	"Ground too hard to work."
Edgar	Garland	E. A. Ewing	158	May 7	Oct. 11	Oct. 18	6	13.3	**11.9**	12.6	17.4	**72.3**	Beets wilted.
Edgar	Paris	D. H. Shank	93	May 14	Oct. 11	Oct. 13	6	18.0	**12.4**	13.1	16.9	**77.5**	....

TABLE 1.—CONTINUED.

Fifty-eight samples from sixteen counties of Southern Illinois.

County.	Town.	Grower.	Lab. No.	Planted.	Harvested.	Analyzed.	No. analyzed	Average weight, oz.	Per cent. Sugar in beets.	Per cent. Sugar in juice.	Per cent. Solids in juice.	Purity coefficient.	Remarks.
Calhoun	Brussels	Wm. Pohlman	233	May 15	Oct. 18	Oct. 21	6	18.0	9.9	10.4	14.1	73.8	Fair cultivation.
Calhoun	Michael	John M. Roth	245	June 5	Oct. 19	Oct. 22	6	10.2	8.9	9.4	13.3	70.5	Fair cultivation.
Greene	Whitehall	Chas. Quigley	270	May 21	Oct. 20	Oct. 26	6	10.3	6.4	6.7	11.2	60.0	Poor cultivation.
Greene	Whitehall	T. A. Smith	265	May 20	Oct. 20	Oct. 25	6	12.0	8.3	8.8	12.8	68.4	Injured by live stock.
Greene	Whitehall	Frank Winters	309	May 1	Oct. 23	Oct. 28	6	21.0	10.9	11.5	15.0	76.6	Fair cultivation.
Macoupin	Carlinville	Frank Hoblit	319	May 20	Oct. 27	Oct. 29	6	15.3	9.9	10.4	15.4	67.5	Good cultivation.
Macoupin	Carlinville	O. P. Smith	191	May 14	Oct. 14	Oct. 19	6	15.7	10.8	11.4	17.6	64.5	Fair cultivation.
Macoupin	Plainview	A. Simmocker	346	May 1		Oct. 30	6	17.8	9.7	10.2	14.4	70.6	Good cultivation.
Macoupin	Staunton	C. T. Dripps	210	Apr. 28	Oct. 18	Oct. 20	6	15.7	14.9	15.7	19.9	78.6	Good cultivation.
Macoupin	Staunton	C. T. Dripps	211	Apr. 25	Oct. 18	Oct 20	4	20.0	13.8	14.6	18.4	79.2	Fair cultivation.
Macoupin	Staunton	C. T. Dripps	212	May 6	Oct. 10	Oct. 20	4	17.5	10.7	11.3	15.4	73.2	Fair cultivation.
Montgomery	Chapman	Jno. Hillman	94	May 25	Oct. 11	Oct. 14	6	6.7	18.6	19.6	23.7	82.6	Injured by bugs.
Montgomery	Donnellson	Geo. W. Wilson	129	Apr. 11	Oct. 12	Oct. 14	6	20.2	13.4	14.1	18.4	76.5	
Montgomery	Farmersville	S. E. Simonson	257	May 20	Oct. 20	Oct. 23	6	15.5	11.0	11.6	14.9	77.8	Poor cultivation.
Montgomery	Irving	Frank Rucker	147	May 7	Oct. 12	Oct. 15	5	28.4	11.6	12.3	16.3	75.3	
Montgomery	Walshville	T. T. Smith	256	May 22	Oct. 21	Oct. 23	6	22.2	10.5	11.1	15.3	72.5	Fair cultivation.
Effingham	Edgewood	Sam'l Bartley	67	Apr. 27	Oct. 7	Oct. 9	6	9.5	12.6	13.3	17.8	74.6	
Clark	Marshall	G. Bamesbarger	72	May 15	Oct. 1	Oct. 11	6	15.8	13 5	14.3	19.8	72.1	Fair cultivation.
Clark	Marshall	Hugo Faust	123	May 25	Oct. 11	Oct. 14	6	9.3	11.7	12.3	17.2	71.4	Fair cultivation.
Clark	Marshall	J. H. Maurer	163		Oct. 12	Oct. 17	4	10.5	12.6	13.3	18.4	72.0	Injured by bugs.
Clark	Martinsville	Austin Sweet	153	May 10	Oct. 13	Oct. 16	7	7.0	16.6	17.5	21.9	80.1	Poor cultivation.
Madison	Alton	Alex Wise	395	June 17	Oct. 29	Nov. 12	6	19.8	11.8	12.5	16.4	76.1	
Madison	Edwardsville	C. W. Fangenroth	223	Apr. 20	Oct. 18	Oct. 20	6	22.5	11.3	11.9	14.9	79.7	Injured by bugs.
Madison	Highland	Albert Luehm	258	May 1	Oct. 18	Oct. 23	6	26.8	9.8	10.4	14.5	71.3	
Madison	Highland	Lorenz Marxer	220	May 1	Oct. 15	Oct. 20	6	23.8	15.3	16.1	19.4	82.7	Poor cultivation.
Madison	Highland	Jacob Mueller	230	May 1		Oct. 21	6	14.2	13.2	13.9	18.6	74.7	Good cultivation.
Madison	Mitchell	H. Brant	86	May 7	Oct. 9	Oct. 12	6	24.7	10.4	10.9	14.2	76.7	Fair cultivation.

Madison	Mitchell	H. Brant	403	May	7	Nov.	12	Nov.	16	6	11.7	**11.7**	12.3	15.6	**79.1**	Fair cultivation.
Madison	Mitchell	L. Hess	87	May	5	Oct.	9	Oct.	12	6	29.8	**8.0**	8.5	12.2	**69.4**	Poor cultivation.
Madison	Mitchell	L. Hess	404	May	5	Nov.	9	Nov.	16	6	11.3	**7.4**	7.8	12.5	**62.3**	Poor cultivation.
Madison	Mitchell	Chas. Lexow	88	Apr.	28	Oct.	9	Oct.	12	6	30.8	**8.3**	8.8	12.6	**69.6**	Fair cultivation.
Madison	Mitchell	Chas. Lexow	406	Apr.	28	Nov.	12	Nov.	16	6	19.2	**8.5**	9.0	12.6	**70.9**	Fair cultivation.
Madison	Mitchell	M. S. Link	89	May	6	Oct.	9	Oct.	12	6	21.5	**7.2**	7.6	11.3	**67.5**	Beets injured by insects.
Madison	Mitchell	M. S. Link	405	May	6	Nov.	12	Nov.	16	6	13.8	**10.6**	11.2	14.7	**76.5**	Beets injured by insects.
Madison	Mitchell	Fr. Troeckler	85	May	10	Oct.	9	Oct.	12	6	25.0	**10.2**	10.7	14.1	**75.9**	Fair cultivation.
Madison	Mitchell	Fr. Troeckler	268	May	3	Oct.	23	Oct.	26	5	22.6	**10.7**	11.3	14.5	**78.2**	Fair cultivation.
Bond	Mulberry Grove	W. A. Elam	228	Apr.	26	Oct.	18	Oct.	20	6	18.0	**10.3**	10.8	13.4	**80.8**	Good cultivation.
St. Clair	Belleville	Jacob Voelinger	214	May	4	Oct.	18	Oct.	20	6	22.3	**12.6**	13.3	17.1	**77.6**	Injured by bugs.
St. Clair	Imbs	Louis Dyroff	198	May	10	Oct.	16	Oct.	19	4	21.3	**13.8**	14.5	17.9	**81.0**	Good cultivation.
St. Clair	Lebanon	Frank Roeder	119	May	11	Oct.	11	Oct.	14	6	23.2	**9.7**	10.2	13.7	**74.3**	Good cultivation.
St. Clair	Mascoutah	L. B. Eidmann	231	May	15	Oct.	7	Oct.	21	6	25.7	**12.8**	13.5	17.1	**78.9**	Beets wilted.
St. Clair	O'Fallon	John Koch	252	May	4	Oct.	15	Oct.	22	6	23.3	**11.1**	11.7	15.7	**74.1**	Good cultivation.
St. Clair	O'Fallon	H. Niebruegge	254	May	3	Oct.	14	Oct.	22	6	23.8	**14.5**	15.3	18.9	**80.6**	Good cultivation.
St. Clair	O'Fallon	H. Oberneufemann	253	May	27	Oct.	16	Oct.	11	6	18.0	**9.7**	10.2	13.6	**74.8**	Fair cultivation.
St. Clair	O'Fallon	Chas. Reiss	251	May	15	Oct.	15	Oct.	19	6	17.3	**10.3**	10.9	15.4	**70.3**	Good cultivation.
St. Clair	O'Fallon	Gustav Schilling	250	May	15	Oct.	1	Oct.	22	6	22.7	**12.2**	12.8	16.0	**79.8**	Good cultivation.
St. Clair	O'Fallon	John H. Weil	248	June	12	Oct.	15	Oct.	22	6	16.8	**13.2**	13.9	17.5	**79.3**	Fair cultivation.
St. Clair	O'Fallon	John H. Weil	249	......		......		Oct.	22	6	12.3	**16.2**	17.1	20.3	**84.1**	Fair cultivation.
Washington	Beaucoup	J. L. Haum	242	May	1	Oct.	18	Oct.	22	6	16.0	**11.9**	12.6	16.7	**75.2**	Beets wilted.
Jefferson	Divide	S. Halbrook	247	May	12	Oct.	19	Oct.	22	6	14.2	**12.1**	12.7	15.0	**85.0**	Fair cultivation.
Wayne	Barnhill	Harry Wilson	358	May	31	Oct.	14	Nov.	3	3	16.3	**14.3**	15.1	19.6	**77.0**	Beets much wilted.
Clay	Bible Grove	Mayfield Smith	244	Apr.	15	Oct.	18	Oct.	22	6	14.5	**11.8**	12.4	18.2	**68.3**	Good cultivation.
Edwards	Bone Gap	Wm. Newberry	264	May	1	Oct.	20	Oct.	25	6	15.2	**8.7**	9.2	15.6	**58.7**	Injured by bugs.
Jackson	Fountain Bluff	H. H. Vogt	243	May	15	Sept.	30	Oct.	23	6	16.3	**10.9**	11.5	15.2	**75.8**	Beets wilted.
Jackson	Pomona	R. S Fuller	66	Apr.	20	Oct.	6	Oct.	9	6	16.8	**10.7**	11.3	15.6	**71.9**	Good cultivation.
Saline	Eldorado	Philip Genter	183	May	15	Oct.	9	Oct.	18	5	9.8	**7.9**	8.3	12.2	**68.1**	Injured by hogs.
Saline	Eldorado	Philip Genter	218	May	15	Oct.	9	Oct.	20	6	8.0	**9.1**	9.6	12.8	**75.1**	Injured by hogs.
Saline	Long Branch	B. A. Durham	353	May	..	Oct.	27	Nov.	2	6	11.3	**11.0**	11.6	18.1	**63.7**	Beets wilted.

In spite of instructions to the contrary growers in many cases planted but a single row, and in a few cases the rows were as much as three or four feet apart. These methods tend to produce beets with a low per cent. of sugar. It is probable that cultivations noted as "good" varied greatly.

Results from the beets grown on the Experiment Station Farm, 1897.

The results shown in table 2 were obtained from beets planted May 11th. It will be observed that the Original Klein Wanzleben makes the best showing, averaging over one pound in weight, about 15 per cent. sugar in the beets, and 85 purity coefficient. The Improved Klein Wanzleben and the Short French gave very satisfactory results, while the Long French were of only medium quality.

It should be understood, however, that these results are from a single year's experiments, and are not to be considered as final.

TABLE 2. ANALYSES OF SUGAR BEETS FROM STATION FARM, VARIETY TESTS.

Laboratory No.	Harvested.	Analyzed.	Ave. Wt. oz.	Per cent. Sugar in beets	Sugar in juice.	Solids in juice.	Purity coefficient.	Variety.
341	Oct. 29	Oct. 30	13.0	15.5	16.3	19.1	85.3	Klein Wanzleben.
385	Nov. 5	Nov. 6	14.8	14.8	15.6	18.4	84.8	Klein Wanzleben.
386	Nov. 5	Nov. 6	23.7	14.3	15.1	17.9	84.5	Klein Wanzleben.
Ave....			17.2	14.9	15.7	18.5	84.9	Klein Wanzleben.
342	Oct. 29	Oct. 30	16.3	13.6	14.3	17.4	82.2	Imp. Klein Wanzleben.
387	Nov. 5	Nov. 6	14.5	14.1	14.8	17.2	86 2	Imp. Klein Wanzleben.
388	Nov. 5	Nov. 6	18.3	13.7	14.5	17.0	85.3	Imp. Klein Wanzleben.
Ave....			16.4	13.8	14.5	17.2	84.6	Imp. Klein Wanzleben.
343	Oct. 29	Oct. 30	12.5	12.9	13.6	16.5	82.0	Short French.
389	Nov. 5	Nov. 6	14.3	13.7	14.5	17.0	85.3	Short French.
390	Nov. 5	Nov. 6	17.2	12.8	13.5	15.9	84.9	Short French.
Ave....			14.7	13.1	13.9	16.5	84.1	Short French.
344	Oct. 29	Oct. 30	11.6	11.0	11.6	14.5	80.0	Long French.
391	Nov. 5	Nov. 6	13.5	12.6	13.3	16.2	82.3	Long French.
392	Nov. 5	Nov. 6	17.0	10.5	11.0	13.8	80.0	Long French.
Ave....			14.0	11.4	12.0	14.8	80.8	Long French.

Difficulty was experienced in selecting samples from a growing crop that should prove to be typical ones after the crop was fully matured. As a matter of fact, the earlier specimens proved to be too small, and uniform weights were not secured. There is therefore more increase in sugar content during the later days of maturity than the tables would indicate.

Upon the matter of season, it may be said that if 1897 was in any way peculiar as regards beets it was because of abnormally low rainfall in August, a circumstance that was unfavorable rather than otherwise to both yield and quality. A table of meteorological data is appended (p. 5) for the benefit of those desiring to make a comparison of seasons.

Table 3 shows the results obtained from an experiment to determine the quality of the beets at different times of harvesting. The plat one by six rods selected for the experiment had been planted May 21st with the Original Klein Wanzleben variety.

The first samples were harvested and analyzed September 14th, samples being taken thereafter at regular intervals of one week for a period of ten weeks. Four samples of five beets each were taken at each time.

GENERAL REMARKS ON THE RESULTS OF THE EXPERIMENTS OF 1897.

To make an average of the results of all samples analyzed or even of all samples from any special section would be manifestly misleading, because every sample must be studied by itself, and in the light of all data given regarding conditions under which the beets were grown.

It may be said, however, that the season's experiments demonstrate conclusively that it is possible to produce beets of excellent quality in all of the general sections of the state. In most cases the beets returned for analysis were above the grade required for factory use, and where this is not the case the reason for the poor quality is usually clearly apparent from the data at hand regarding the conditions under which the beets were grown.

INJURIES.

A few cases of injury by insects have been reported, all by the striped potato beetle (not the Colorado beetle) or by the false chinch bug (*Nysius Angustatus*) and not the true chinch bug which is limited to the grass family. Experience in Nebraska has found the crop to be peculiarly free from insect and fungus injuries.

ILLINOIS AS A SUGAR PRODUCING STATE.

A variety of conditions determine the sugar producing capacity of a state. The business is one calling for expensive manufacturing plants and for most intensive methods in agriculture. While the plant should be so established as to admit of expansion, yet from the nature of the business it cannot begin on a small scale and establish itself by degrees as conditions improve and experience is gained. It must begin full-fledged and the magnitude of the enterprise, even at the minimum, and the variety of the interests involved, admit of few mistakes and no positively unfavorable conditions. Every circumstance bearing upon

TABLE 3. ANALYSES OF SUGAR BEETS FROM STATION FARM, TIME OF HARVEST.

Laboratory No.	Harvested and analyzed.	Ave. wt. oz.	Per cent.			Purity coefficient.
			Sugar in beets.	Sugar in juice.	Solids in juice.	
1	Sept. 14	10.8	**13.2**	13.9	16.8	**82.5**
2	Sept. 14	10.6	**13.8**	14.6	17.5	**83.1**
3	Sept. 14	8.8	**13.7**	14.4	16.8	**85.6**
4	Sept. 14	9.2	**13.4**	14.1	16.7	**84.1**
Average	....	9.9	**13.5**	14.3	17.0	**83.8**
5	Sept. 21	11.2	**14.1**	14.8	17.9	**82.9**
6	Sept. 21	9.4	**14.7**	15.5	18.2	**85.0**
7	Sept. 21	7.6	**13.4**	14.1	17.2	**82.3**
8	Sept. 21	9.2	**13.7**	14.4	17.2	**84.0**
Average ..	....	9.4	**14.0**	14.7	17.6	**83.6**
9	Sept. 28	9.4	**14.1**	14.8	17.8	**83.2**
10	Sept. 28	12.8	**13.6**	14.3	17.3	**82.6**
11	Sept. 28	9.4	**13.7**	14.4	16.9	**85.1**
12	Sept. 28	10.0	**14.8**	15.5	18.2	**85.4**
Average	....	10.4	**14.1**	14.8	17.6	**84.1**
13	Oct. 5	10.8	**15.3**	16.1	19.2	**83.5**
14	Oct. 5	14.2	**14.9**	15.7	18.9	**83.0**
15	Oct. 5	12.6	**13.6**	14.3	17.1	**83.6**
16	Oct. 5	12.0	**14.5**	15.3	18.2	**84.1**
Average	....	12.4	**14.6**	15.4	18.4	**83.6**
17	Oct. 12	12.6	**13.2**	13.9	16.7	**83.4**
18	Oct. 12	14.6	**13.4**	14.1	16.7	**84.2**
19	Oct. 12	12.8	**14.0**	14.8	17.3	**85.1**
20	Oct. 12	13.2	**14.3**	15.0	17.6	**85.1**
Average ...	....	13.3	**13.7**	14.5	17.1	**84.5**
21	Oct. 19	13.8	**13.6**	14.4	17.3	**83.0**
22	Oct. 19	12.0	**15.2**	16.0	19.1	**83.8**
23	Oct. 19	19.6	**14.2**	14.9	17.4	**85.6**
24	Oct. 19	16.6	**14.0**	14.7	17.3	**85.0**
Average	....	15.5	**14.3**	15.0	17.8	**84.4**
25	Oct. 26	12.6	**14.3**	15.1	18.0	**83.8**
26	Oct. 26	13.4	**13.4**	14.1	17.0	**83.1**
27	Oct. 26	9.8	**14.2**	14.9	17.5	**85.2**
28	Oct. 26	13.4	**14.0**	14.8	16.7	**88.6**
Average	....	12.3	**14.0**	14.7	17.3	**85.2**
29	Nov. 2	13.0	**13.5**	14.3	17.4	**81.9**
30	Nov. 2	15.6	**13.8**	14.6	17.5	**83.2**
31	Nov. 2	12.6	**14.7**	15.5	18.4	**84.2**
32	Nov. 2	15.6	**14.7**	15.5	17.9	**86.6**
Average	....	14.2	**14.2**	15.0	17.8	**84.0**
33	Nov. 9	14.8	**14.1**	14.9	17.9	**82.8**
34	Nov. 9	12.8	**16.1**	16.9	19.8	**85.3**
35	Nov. 9	13.6	**15.3**	16.1	18.8	**85.6**
36	Nov. 9	12.8	**15.4**	16.2	18.6	**87.0**
Average	....	13.5	**15.2**	16.0	18.8	**85.2**
37	Nov. 16	19.2	**14.3**	15.0	17.6	**85.5**
38	Nov. 16	19.8	**13.4**	14.1	17.0	**82.9**
39	Nov. 16	17.8	**14.3**	15.1	17.8	**84.8**
40	Nov. 16	19.2	**14.4**	15.2	18.1	**84.1**
Average ...	....	19.0	**14.1**	14.9	17.6	**84.3**

TABLE 4 ANALYSES OF SUGAR BEETS FROM STATION FARM. DEPTH OF PLOWING.

Laboratory No.	Harvested.	Analyzed.	Average wt. oz.	Per cent. Sugar in beets.	Sugar in juice.	Solids in juice.	Purity coefficient.	
26	Oct. 26	Oct. 26	13.4	**13.4**	14.1	17.0	**83.1**	Plowed 8 inches.
28	Oct. 26	Oct 26	13.4	**14.0**	14.8	16.7	**88.6**	Plowed 8 inches.
30	Nov. 2	Nov. 2	15.6	**13.8**	14.6	17.5	**83.2**	Plowed 8 inches.
32	Nov. 2	Nov. 2	15.6	**14.7**	15.5	17.9	**86.6**	Plowed 8 inches.
Ave....			14.5	**14.0**	14.8	17.3	**85.4**	Plowed 8 inches.
327	Oct. 29	Oct. 29	14.7	**15.5**	16.3	18.8	**86.9**	Plowed 10 inches.
328	Oct. 29	Oct. 29	12.8	**15.9**	16.8	19.7	**85.2**	Plowed 10 inches.
359	Nov. 2	Nov. 3	12.8	**15.2**	16.0	18.8	**85.1**	Plowed 10 inches.
360	Nov. 2	Nov. 3	20 2	**14.0**	14.8	17.4	**84.8**	Plowed 10 inches.
Ave ...			15.1	**15.2**	16.0	18.7	**85.5**	Plowed 10 inches.
325	Oct. 29	Oct. 29	18.3	**14.4**	15.2	18.5	**82.2**	Subsoiled 16 inches.
326	Oct. 29	Oct. 29	12.7	**14.6**	15.4	18.4	**83.7**	Subsoiled 16 inches.
361	Nov. 2	Nov. 3	14.7	**14.7**	15.5	19.0	**81.6**	Subsoiled 16 inches.
362	Nov. 2	Nov. 3	20.7	**14.0**	14.8	17.9	**82.4**	Subsoiled 16 inches.
Ave....			16.6	**14.4**	15.2	18.5	**82.5**	Subsoiled 16 inches.

These beets were grown from Improved Klein Wanzleben seed, planted May 21st. The results show no marked influence from the different depths of plowing, the lower purity coefficient of the samples from the subsoiled plat being the most noticeable.

TABLE 5. ANALYSES OF SUGAR BEETS FROM STATION FARM. DISTANCE BETWEEN ROWS.

Laboratory No.	Harvested.	Analyzed.	Average wt. oz.	Per cent. Sugar in beets.	Sugar in juice.	Solids in juice.	Purity coefficient.	Distance between rows.
329	Oct. 29	Oct. 30	11.5	**16.6**	17.5	20.6	**84.8**	15 inches.
363	Nov. 2	Nov. 3	14.0	**15.1**	15.9	18.7	**85.0**	15 inches.
364	Nov. 2	Nov. 3	21.2	**13.5**	14.2	16.8	**84.1**	15 inches.
Ave.......			15.6	**15.1**	15.9	18.7	**84.6**	15 inches.
330	Oct. 29	Oct. 30	13.7	**14.4**	15.2	18.5	**82.2**	18 inches.
365	Nov. 2	Nov. 3	14.7	**15.4**	16.2	19.3	**84.2**	18 inches.
366	Nov. 2	Nov. 3	20.8	**13.9**	14.6	17.9	**81.8**	18 inches.
Ave.......			16.4	**14.6**	15.3	18.6	**82.7**	18 inches.
331	Oct. 29	Oct. 30	16.8	**13.1**	13.8	17.1	**80.7**	22 inches.
367	Nov. 2	Nov. 3	15.5	**13.7**	14.5	17.9	**81.0**	22 inches.
368	Nov. 2	Nov. 3	20.0	**14.0**	14.7	17.4	**84.4**	22 inches.
Ave.......			17.4	**13.6**	14.3	17.5	**82.0**	22 inches.
332	Oct. 29	Oct. 30	16.8	**12.1**	12.7	16.1	**79.0**	28 inches.
369	Nov. 2	Nov. 3	13.7	**12.5**	13.2	16.2	**81.1**	28 inches.
370	Nov. 2	Nov. 3	18.3	**12.4**	13.1	16.1	**81.1**	28 inches.
Ave.......			16.3	**12.3**	13	16.1	**80.4**	28 inches.
333	Oct. 29	Oct. 30	14.5	**12.5**	13.2	16.4	**80.5**	36 inches.
334	Oct. 29	Oct. 30	8.4	**13.1**	13.8	17.0	**81.2**	44 inches.

These beets were grown from Original Klein Wanzleben seed, planted May 11th. The results show a very marked influence of the distance between rows. As the distance is increased the per cent. of sugar and the purity coefficient decrease. By reference to Nos. 333 and 334 it will be observed that even beets of small size are of comparatively poor quality when grown in rows wide apart.

the success of such an enterprise should be known and estimated as far as possible in advance. Moreover, because of the bulk of the crop and the cost of transportation, the factory must be situated very near the beet producing region, and may not, as in the flouring business, be located in a distant city. This brings grower and manufacturer close together and affords opportunity for endless friction. Here is large capital tied up in an expensive plant that is idle for two-thirds of the year yet seeking profitable returns in amounts so great as to attract attention among the growers, some of whom through ignorance or other cause are certain to incur heavy losses. Friendly relations between these diverse interests are absolutely essential to success, and they can be maintained only when the most exact information generally prevails touching every detail. No mistakes must be made in choosing location, in drawing contracts between grower and factory, or in the process of growing, or of manufacturing. At the outset, therefore, no item involved is too trivial for careful consideration, and before this new enterprise comes into the state every factor, favorable and unfavorable, must be reviewed.

QUALITY OF BEETS.—Experiments conducted during the past season as reported in the tables of this bulletin show conclusively that beets of excellent quality may be produced in all the general sections of the state. It is not surprising that some of the samples analyzed were below grade when it is remembered that often the beets were grown in single rows and always without expert knowledge of the needs of the crop. As conditions were, nearly every locality returned many excellent beets, and it is not too much to conclude that the soil and climate of Illinois are eminently adapted to the growth of an excellent quality of beet. This would seem to be at variance with the experience at Chatsworth and Freeport some 30 to 35 years ago when failure was due to a variety of causes, prominent among which may be mentioned: lack of knowledge of practical details on the part of both grower and manufacturer; lack of support on the part of growers; lack of the improved methods of today. Now, however, the beet has been improved by selection and breeding until it carries a higher per cent. of sugar, and with the diffusion process, the relative amount of sugar recovered is vastly greater than before. Under present conditions the deep prairie soils are even preferable to sandy soils, because of increased yield, and the sugar industry is coming into the richer lands.

YIELD.—There is abundant proof that Illinois can produce large yields of beets. Ten to fourteen tons per acre of marketable beets were grown the past season at the Station farm under ordinary treatment, with no special tools and upon land that has been cropped for many years. Reports of much higher yields have come from many sections of the state. While 12½ tons per acre would be a fair average for Illinois, no good farmer would be satisfied with less than 15 tons. Experience confirms the statement that with beets, as with other crops, other things equal, the better the soil the better the yield; and there is every reason to know that the rich prairie soils of Illinois are especially adapted to heavy yields of sugar beets. But they must be crowded until the individual beets are reduced in size from a possible ten or twelve pounds to the proper weight of one and a half to two pounds.

LABOR.—Beets cannot be raised with the tools or the methods that are successful with Indian corn. After making use of the best special machinery there yet remains a large amount of hand labor, and this must be performed in case of large areas not by the regular force upon the farm, but by a larger number employed for the special purpose. This calls for an additional force of laborers during the growing and harvesting seasons, and indicates the neighborhood of a city or a considerable town as the most likely source of the hand labor involved in the production of a crop of sugar beets. It would be little else than folly to undertake the growth of beets on a commercial scale, except by aid of such labor as has been indicated, and even then good management will be needed to keep the cost of production down to the standard of $32.00 per acre.

COAL AND LIME.—Large quantities of both coal and lime are imperative for factory use, and the nearer the actual supply the less the cost of transportation.

There are 874 coal mines in the state with a yearly output of something over seventeen million tons. This abundant supply of soft coal over nearly all the state south of the Illinois river, together with excellent facilities for cheap transportation over railroads free from heavy grades, brings the cost exceedingly low and prices range from a dollar a ton up.

Almost any coal will answer the purpose, but the lime must be comparatively free from soluble minerals, because soluble salts in either lime or water have the same effect as when in beets, which is to prevent the crystallization, and therefore to cause the loss of nearly or quite their full equivalent of sugar. The state is nearly everywhere underlaid by coal and lime, but in the absence of a state agricultural and economic survey a letter of inquiry, touching the Illinois supply of coal and lime was addressed by the Director to Professor C. W. Rolfe, Geologist of the University. His reply is quoted in full.

URBANA, Jan. 19, 1898.

Professor E. Davenport,

Director Experiment Station,

DEAR SIR:—Referring to your recent inquiry regarding the limestone and coal deposits of our state which could be made available for the manufacture of sugar from beets, will say, I deeply regret my inability to give you the *specific* information you desire.

The geologic investigations which have heretofore been undertaken by the state were confined almost exclusively to stratigraphy and paleontology, leaving our natural resources practically untouched. I earnestly hope this will be remedied in the near future.

First as to coal. If a line be drawn from Danville, Vermilion County, through Paxton, Ford County, Wilmington, Will County, Rock Island, Rock Island County, thence south following the general direction of the Mississippi, but at a distance of say 25 miles eastward to the north line of Union County, thence east to the state line, all counties, with very few exceptions, included in the enclosed area, would be able to furnish coal of suitable quality and in sufficient quantity to meet all probable demands, and to counties without this area our many lines of railroad are able to supply coal almost as cheaply.

Second as to limestone. Very few analyses of Illinois limestones have been made, but basing an opinion on these, and a considerable field acquaintance with the rocks of the state, I do not hesitate to express the opinion that accessible deposits which will meet your requirements, can be found in at least four-fifths of the counties. I append a short list of *typical* outcrops which I feel sure would meet your demands.

Trenton Limestone (Blue), Galena, Jo Daviess County.
Trenton Limestone, Thebes, Alexander County.
Niagara Limestone, Grafton, Jersey County.
Niagara Limestone, Joliet, Will County.
Hamilton Limestone (Gray), Rock Island County.
Oriskany Limestone, Jackson County.
Burlington Limestone, Gladstone, Henderson County.
Burlington Limestone, Quincy, Adams County.
Keokuk Limestone, Nauvoo, Hancock County.
St. Louis Limestone, Rosiclare, Hardin County.
Chester Limestone, Chester, Randolph County.

There are also many deposits in the coal measures which would be suited to this use.

Respectfully submitted,

C. W. ROLFE, *Professor of Geology*.

WATER.—Immense quantities of water are required at the factory for washing beets, and this may be afforded by a river or a small stream. The most cursory glance at the map will show the state to be abundantly supplied with running water. But for the work of diffusion an abundant supply of comparatively pure water is required, and the following letter is in reply to a request for explicit information concerning the character of the water supply of the state:

UNIVERSITY OF ILLINOIS, January 20, 1898.

Professor Eugene Davenport,

Director Agricultural Experiment Station,

DEAR SIR:—In reply to your query regarding the water supplies of Illinois with respect to the use of water in the manufacture of sugar from beets, I would say that in most regions of the state water that is sufficiently pure for this purpose is available. In some districts of the state waters drawn from the deeper wells are charged with a considerable amount of chlorides and, in some cases, of sulphates; but through most of the sections of the state waters drawn from drift wells and also those drawn from wells in rock are comparatively free from sulphates or chlorides, the mineral matters consisting mainly of carbonates of calcium and magnesium, and would be well suited to use in the manufacture of beet sugar. Some deeper drift wells yield waters which are charged with considerable quantities of organic matters, but these are present in less quantity than is commonly found in surface water, that is, river and lake waters; consequently in my opinion they would be serviceable in this manufacture.

Yours very truly,

ARTHUR W. PALMER,
Professor of Chemistry.

TRANSPORTATION AND MARKETS.—Besides enjoying the advantages of four navigable rivers, Illinois is better supplied with railroads than is any other state in the Union. One hundred and nine separate lines are operated within the state with an aggregate length of over 10,500 miles, and with 2,740 stations. This vast mileage is in the hands of about sixty great companies whose trunk lines communicate with the East, and with the West, with the Great Lakes, and with the Gulf, and focus at the great trade centers, Chicago and St. Louis. Of the 102 counties of the state, but three are without railroad facilities; two of these lie upon the Ohio river and one between the Mississippi and the Illinois.

ADVANTAGES UNEXCELLED.—With an inexhaustible supply of coal and lime well distributed over the state; with numberless rivers and small streams everywhere, and with an abundance of excellent well-water; with unequalled river and railroad transportation; with easy and direct access to two of the greatest trade centers, and with its natural relations to both the Gulf and the Great Lakes, it would seem that Illinois possesses ideal factory conditions.

That the soil and the climate of Illinois are adapted to the production of large yields of beets of excellent quality is abundantly shown by the experiments of the past year, which are held to be conclusive for the northern and central sections, and for a large portion of the southern section.

While the laboring population of the state is at present located with reference to other industries, there is every reason to suppose that in Illinois as elsewhere it would be attracted to the beet fields at the proper season. The neighborhood of the larger coal mines would furnish ideal conditions for hand labor in beet raising.

WHAT REMAINS TO BE DONE.—But one thing remains, and that is the education of the people in the details of a new industry, with all that this implies. The people who are to grow beets must learn how to produce profitable crops from the very first, and friendly relations must be established and maintained between grower and factory in order that temporary or permanent failure may be averted. Experience elsewhere has shown the importance of a good start, and the disaster of hasty procedure at the outset; it has everywhere demonstrated the *absolute necessity of accurate knowledge well diffused throughout the community.*

The growing of sugar beets is eminently intensive agriculture. The methods and machinery with which our people are best acquainted and the experience gained from growing corn will not avail. Many of the fundamentals are entirely opposite, as for example, that the largest beet is not the best one. The business needs special tools, special methods, and special attention. Large values will go into the crop at best, and, if not well bestowed, loss will surely follow, and the grower will tend to blame either the business or the factory.

It is not that the beet sugar business is extremely hazardous, nor that the margin of profit is narrow. Well conducted, the business is very profitable to both grower and manufacturer under anything like present conditions. But our people are not as yet acquainted with intensive agriculture, and the necessary heavy outlay per acre. Neither are our farmers accustomed to close contact with extensive manufacturing plants employing large capital. This new knowledge must be gained and these new relations become habitual, and nothing but the most careful and concerted action will quickly and smoothly accomplish the end.

WHAT IS NEEDED.—Not state bounty, nor public patronage, but united community interest, and detailed information. The present tariff makes conditions exceedingly favorable for the introduction of this new industry into the United States, and experience has shown that to enlist public favor in the way of bounty or other advantage is not only unnecessary under present favorable trade conditions, but that it only serves, speedily to draw down upon the infant industry the public wrath, and to introduce a third party that is disposed to assume the attitude of a beguiled and disaffected patron. The business needs not special favor but special care and special knowledge, and this care must be observed, and this knowledge must be acquired by the growers themselves.

Moreover, individual exertion is of little moment except to arouse and engage the community or at least enough of the community to support a factory. This factory should be built with a view to enlargement as the business expands, but it must not be built upon the smallest possible plan for then the expense of management will surely absorb all profits. In all this matter the community must organize and work together, and when once the contracts are drawn every man should render loyal support to the capital that has been invested.

COST AND PROFIT IN GROWING BEETS.

When it became apparent that beets of good quality could be produced in Illinois the writer was authorized to visit Grand Island and Norfolk, Nebraska, to secure the most trustworthy information possible relative to the commercial success of the industry. This question must be considered in the light of both the grower and the manufacturer, for the interests between them must necessarily be mutual. Neither can succeed without the other, consequently there must be a profit for both; and unless these profits can be shown to be comparatively large from the outset, neither the farmer nor the capitalist, if judicious, will venture upon a new industry in which, at best, experience must be gained at the expense of profits. Nor will they continue in the business, if from want of proper methods, or other causes, the first experiences are disastrous.

Through the kindness of Manager Ferrar of the Grand Island Factory, the Station is able to insert the following contract which is the basis of operations at both the Nebraska factories, and does not differ materially from those in use at other American factories:

To raise rich beets it is absolutely necessary to have a full stand, therefore you cannot plant too much seed. It is unadvisable to silo beets before October 15th, but all beets if ripe should be in silo by November 1st.

FARMER'S CONTRACT TO FACTORY.

..........Acres.

No.......... ....189....

For and in consideration of One Dollar, in hand paid, receipt whereof is hereby acknowledged, I,........................, do hereby agree with the Oxnard Beet Sugar Co. to plant, cultivate and harvest to the best of my ability and in a husband-like manner..........acres of sugar beets on the farm occupied by me, located....
....
in Section.... ...., Township..............., Range................
County of..................., and upon the following terms and conditions, viz:

That seed or planting the aforesaid acreage is to be furnished to me at 15 cents per pound F.O.B. Grand Island, and I hereby agree that I will not sell or give away any such seed, and that I will deliver all beets grown therefrom at the factory at such times as agreed upon in this contract, with tops closely and squarely cut off at the base of bottom leaf, said beets to be free from dirt and in a marketable condition, for the sum of $4.00 per ton, provided, however, that said beets shall contain not less than 12 per cent. sugar to the weight of the beet with a purity coefficient of 80, and the sum of $4 00 per ton will also be paid for all beets containing not less than 14 per cent. sugar regardless of purity and for all beets of 13 per cent. sugar and a purity coefficient not lower than 78.

That all seed furnished for the replanting of beets under this contract shall be at a price of 15 cents per pound, F. O. B. Grand Island, and the amount due for seed shall be paid for by me in cash or be deducted from the first payment for beets delivered.

That to secure a full stand I will plant on the acreage specified all the seed furnished by the Oxnard Beet Sugar Co., same not to exceed twenty pounds per acre.

That all beets must be kept free from frost, it being distinctly understood that the Oxnard Beet Sugar Co. will only accept beets that are in a sound condition at the time of shipment.

That beets are to be delivered at the option of the Oxnard Beet Sugar Co. upon reasonable notice from the Company, on its order, at any time prior to October 15th. After that date the Oxnard Beet Sugar Co. shall have the option of ordering in beets as they may require, provided, however, that they order for shipment of the beets so grown, in all, not less than four tons of beets per acre of the acreage to be harvested, previous to the 5th day of November, 1898, and not less than six tons per acre previous to the 1st day of January, 1899, and not less than eight tons per acre previous to the 1st day of February, 1899, and all the remainder previous to the 20th day of February, 1899.

That should any beets grown under this contract fail to come up to the above standards for which $4 00 per ton is to be paid, they will then be paid for at the following scheduled prices:

For all Beets containing not less than	
13 per cent. sugar and a purity coefficient of 76, 12 per cent. sugar and a purity coefficient of 79,	$3.75 per ton.
13 per cent. sugar and a purity coefficient of 75, 12 per cent. sugar and a purity coefficient of 78,	$3.50 per ton.
13 per cent. sugar and a purity coefficient of 74, 12 per cent. sugar and a purity coefficient of 76, 11 per cent. sugar and a purity coefficient of 78,	$3.25 per ton.
13 per cent. sugar and a purity coefficient of 73, 12 per cent. sugar and a purity coefficient of 74, 11 per cent. sugar and a purity coefficient of 75,	$3.00 per ton.
For all Beets below 13 per cent. sugar and a purity coefficient of 73, 12 per cent. sugar and a purity coefficient of 74, 11 per cent. sugar and a purity coefficient of 75,	$2.50 per ton.

However, no beets will be received at the factory containing less than 10.5 per cent. sugar and a purity coefficient of 73.

It being distinctly understood that said low grade beets shall not be delivered by me until after the Oxnard Beet Sugar Co. shall have worked up all beets that reach the required standard of 12 per cent. of sugar with a purity of 80, unless the Oxnard Beet Sugar Co. should otherwise direct, and that said Oxnard Beet Sugar Co. shall not be required to accept any portion of said beets containing less than 10.5 per cent. of sugar and a purity coefficient of 73.

That all analyses made by the Oxnard Beet Sugar Co. shall be accepted as final, it being understood, however, that the farmers are at liberty to select and employ at their own expense any competent chemist to whom the Oxnard Beet Sugar Co. shall give free access to their beet laboratory for the purpose of checking the test made by the chemist of the Oxnard Beet Sugar Co.

That I will notify the Oxnard Beet Sugar Co. after my beets are laid by but not later than August 15th, how many acres of beets I will have to harvest the next fall.

No agent of the Oxnard Beet Sugar Co. has authority to change any of the terms or conditions of this contract.

WITNESS:

....

It should be pointed out here that the terms of the contracts are entirely in the hands of the factories and presumably satisfactory to them. Can the farmer meet the conditions thus imposed by the factories one year with another and have a fair margin of profit left? The following statements are by reliable men whom the writer interviewed personally:

Mr. H. A. Pasewalk, Norfolk, Neb., is an implement dealer who grows beets because there is money in the business. He raised 80 acress of beets in 1896 and 90 acres in 1897. His statement of average cost and profit per acre is as follows:

Plowing	$1.50
Fitting ground and planting	1.50
20 lb. of seed @ 15 cents per lb	3.00
Bunching and thinning	4.50
Two hoeings	4.00
Four cultivations	1.50
Lifting	1.25
Topping	4.00
Hauling 10 tons beets 3 miles	5.00
Siloing one-half of crop	.75
Rent of land	5.00
Total cost per acre	$32.00
Gross receipts from 10 tons of beets @ $4.00 per ton	40.00
Net profit	$8.00

Mr. Edmund Starke, of Grand Island, Nebraska, grows approximately 128 acres each year. The following is the average cost of growing, and profit for the five years from 1892–1897 in which he has been engaged in the business:

Plowing one acre	$ 1.50
Fitting ground and planting	1.00
20 lb. of seed @ 15 cents	3.00
Bunching and thinning	5.00
Four hoeings	5.00
Six cultivations	1.50
Lifting, topping, hauling (3 miles), siloing one-half of crop	10.00
Rent of land	4.00
Total cost for one acre	$32.00
Gross receipts from 12½ tons of beets @ $4.00 per ton	$50.00
Net profit	$18.00

Mr. Henry C. Giese, who has grown beets for the Grand Island Factory since it was erected in 1890, gives the cost and profit per acre for the past season's crop of 25 acres:

Plowing	$ 1.00
Preparing ground	.50
Planting	.50
20 lb. seed @ 15 cents	3.00
Bunching and thinning	4.00
Two hoeings	5.50
Pulling weeds	1.00
Four cultivations	1.00
Lifting, throwing in piles and topping	4.75
Siloing one-half of crop	1.50
Rent of land	6.00
Delivering 12.6 tons one mile @ 25 cents	3.15
Total cost per acre	$31.90
Receipts from 12.6 tons @ $4.00	$50.00
Net profit per acre	$18.10

Yields the past season were lighter than usual. In 1896 Mr. Giese's beets yielded 16½ tons, bringing him $66.00 per acre. In 1895 he raised 19 tons per acre, and owing to the bounty on sugar that year in Nebraska, the factory paid $5.00 per ton, and Mr. Giese received $95.00 per acre. Mr. Giese's corn crop on adjoining land was yielding 50 bushels per acre, which was better than the average, and the market price at that time was 16 cents per bushel, bringing him $8.00 per acre, or a little more than the rent.

The above cases are not exceptional and many others could be cited showing essentially the same results.

The Sass Brothers grew 115 acres this year which yielded 10 tons per acre. They estimate the cost of growing, in case land is rented and all labor hired, at from $26.00 to $30.00 per acre, varying somewhat with the condition of the ground, freedom from weeds, etc. This year they will receive $4,600 for their crop, and will pay out for expenses $1,265, leaving $3,335 for their own labor, rent, etc. They were thoroughly acquainted with the business, and as a consequence expenses were reduced to a minimum.

The crop of 1896 was unusually large, and several railroad agents, traveling men, etc., rented land and went into the business as a speculation. The following is the result of such an investment by Dr. Finch and Wm. Murr, the former a physician, and the latter a traveling man, who rented 128 acres near Grand Island:

Rent of land	$ 5.00
Plowing	1.25
Harrowing, rolling, and planting	1.50
Thinning, bunching and three hoeings	13.50
Pulling and topping	4.50
Lifting	1.25

Siloing if delivering late	2 50
Hauling 10 tons 4 miles @ 70 cents	7.00
Seed 20 lb. @ 15 cents	3.00
Total cost of one acre	$39.50
Receipts from 10 tons @ $4.00	$40.00
Net proceeds	$ .50

These were the only growers whom I met who were not anxious to continue the business.

An opportunity was offered to converse with a large number of beet growers, some at their farms, but more at the factory, as over 200 loads were coming in daily. To the question "Why are you growing beets?" one of three answers was invariably given: 1st. "Because it is the surest crop the farmer can raise;" 2d, "it is a cash crop and the price is practically fixed;" and 3d, "there is more money in it than in any other crop." These statements are borne out by the fact that the beet acreage has so rapidly increased at both the Nebraska factories that there is sharp competition among the farmers to secure contracts for growing beets and either factory could contract for twice the beets it is able to handle. Again, land values and rents have more than doubled since 1891 in the region tributary to both factories.

The exceptionally prosperous condition of the beet sugar sections is well recognized by traveling men. During the past season $160,000 was paid to the farmers of each of the above communities for 40,000 tons of beets, and this does not include the $40,000 paid to local laborers in and about the factories.

As to yields and cost of growing, certainly Illinois will be at no disadvantage. While the average rainfall and temperature for the growing season is about the same as for Grand Island and Norfolk, yet Illinois has much less to fear from drouth and hot destructive winds than has Nebraska. At the Experiment Station under very ordinary conditions the average yield was 12 tons per acre of properly topped beets, ready for the factory. While the reports from growers in all sections show that this is not excessive, yet many have greatly exceeded this amount. In this connection it will be of interest to know that in Germany the average yield is about 12 tons per acre for the whole country.

Wherever the industry has become established in a community in the United States, and the many details of beet culture are understood by the farmers, the profits are comparatively large. But it should be clearly pointed out in this connection that the details of beet culture are many, and must be thoroughly understood. The haphazard methods so often practiced in corn culture would be fatal in the case of beets.

Culture is everything. Excellent beets may be grown on a great variety of soils, but they will not endure poor culture. Poor soil, a hard or wet subsoil, too deep planting, uneven stand, fresh or coarse manure, improper or untimely thinning or weeding, and insufficient cultivation and hoeing are all disastrous to good yield and high sugar content. But the beet sugar industry carries into a community, or rather builds up, better agricultural practices. A careful study of the effects of the industry upon a community brings out clearly the fact that other crops instead of being driven out, are on the contrary, increased in both total production and in yield per acre.

Instructions for Sugar Beet Culture.

The following instructions from the Oxnard Beet Sugar Company are quoted entire as being a brief and most complete statement of the essentials of beet culture. This is especially valuable as it emanates from a commercial source, and is based upon seven years of successful experience under conditions very similar to our own.

SOIL.

Never select poor land. Use the best piece available on your farm, for the richer the soil the better the crop. The best soil is so called bottom land. New land should not be selected, as it never produces a high tonnage—it should be at least two years under cultivation. If possible spread the ground before plowing with well rotted manure. Should there not be sufficient manure at hand, we would advise the use of a fertilizer consisting of lime-cake, ammonia and phosphates. This may perhaps appear to be expensive, but experience has shown that greatly increased tonnage results therefrom. Under no circumstances should seed be planted where land is sandy enough to blow.

PLOWING.

Immediately after taking off the grain, plow shallow (2 or 3 inches) in order to prevent the weeds from going to seed. When this is done spread your field with manure and in the fall plow deep (10 to 12 inches). This is very important, because the beet is thereby enabled to penetrate into the subsoil without much obstruction, thus preventing it from growing out of the ground and allowing it to extract considerable nourishment from the lower soil. The deep plowing will also give you clean ground and will make it ready for early planting and thus insure large tonnage.

In case the plowing has not been done in the fall, *plow as early in the spring* as the ground will do to handle without sticking, *for three reasons:* 1st, because the sooner the weeds are encouraged to grow the more of them can be killed before planting the beets; 2nd, because land plowed while the weather is cool will retain the moisture much longer than it will if plowed during warm weather; 3d because it is much better to allow the ground to settle as much as possible after plowing and before preparation of seed bed so that it will become thoroughly packed, thus insuring better and quicker germination. In the spring never throw up more than two inches of soil that has not been stirred before; if your soil has never been plowed over 6 inches it is better to use a subsoil plow to loosen the ground to the proper depth. These instructions refer only to spring plowing; when good land with deep soil is plowed in the fall, it makes no difference how much new soil is turned up as it would decay in winter through the action of the frost. After spring plowing harrow or better float, once immediately, and then leave the ground as it is *until the time to prepare the seed bed, thus allowing the weeds to sprout.* If the previous crop was corn it is absolutely necessary to take the stalks and roots off the ground in the right manner in order to permit of easy and proper horse-cultivation; it will not do to plow the stalks under, however, as it cannot be done effectually the cultivator-knives bringing them back to the surface once more, and at the same time dragging along with them, more or less of the small beet plants. The best way is to remove the mold-board from the plow which will enable you to loosen the roots without turning the corn stalks under. Then gather them up with a hay rake into piles and after burning as much as possible haul off the remainder.

PREPARATION OF SEED BED.

Land that has been fall-plowed must be harrowed as soon as the frost is out of the ground and the soil is dry enough to prevent sticking. This work will level the

BEET DRILL.

ground, thereby holding the moisture in the soil and increase the germination of the weeds, etc. To secure a good crop, it is absolutely necessary to kill all the weeds in the ground before seeding. *Here is where most failures occur*, and if weeds are allowed to get a start the cultivation of the crop will involve much unnecessary and expensive hand-work. *Therefore, to prepare a good seed-bed*, we advise working the soil four to five inches deep with a pulverizer, or better yet with a corn cultivator, once lengthwise and once crosswise, making sure not to miss any spot in the field as it is necessary to loosen any weeds that may have already sprouted. Then harrow lengthwise and crosswise to level the soil perfectly and finish killing the weeds. After this pack the top soil (2 to 3 inches) well, with a heavy roller, never use a plank float, as floated ground is never well packed and will besides increase blowing and washing. The better the soil is packed *after the weeds are killed*, the better the beet seed will sprout. All the above work must be performed at a time when the ground is in good working condition, (that is, not too damp, as the working of wet soil must be strictly avoided). As beet seed requires considerable moisture to germinate it would also be a great loss to the beet-grower to allow the soil during the preparation of the seed bed to dry out; therefore in dry weather or in an average season the field must be prepared and seeded the same day, this being the only way in which the moisture can be kept in the ground—a great feature in crop-raising and especially so in beet-culture.

To prevent blowing, which is very disastrous to the small beet plants, (our experience has shown us, that even the best black bottom land will blow, if level and fine, which it must be to secure a good crop) we advise running a light harrow over the field, after rolling but before seeding. This harrow must be very light and can be easily constructed and without much expense by using 2x2 pine pieces for the beams and large nails for the teeth, only letting them project below the beams 1½ to 2 inches. This harrow must simply scratch the soil (not over ½ inch deep), thus giving a rough surface, which will surely prevent blowing, except on dry, sandy soil, on which, for this reason and some others, sugar beets should never be planted. The soil must not be loosened again by a deep harrowing, as this would injure the germination.

SEEDING.

To secure a full yield it is absolutely necessary to have a good stand. The time of planting depends largely upon the season, it being generally from about

April 25th to May 25th, or about the season of corn planting. Not less than 20 pounds of seed per acre should be used to secure a good stand under all conditions; because, should the weather be dry the best seed will come up first and there will be enough for a good stand; on the other hand should a crust be formed on the field after a heavy rain one plant will help the other to break through the ground. *Therefore sow at least 20 pounds to the acre.*

Seeders made especially for this purpose, seeding four rows at a time and dropping the seed continuously in rows (14 to 18 inches apart, according to the fertility of the soil) will plant 10 to 12 acres per day. *Never plant over three-fourths of an inch deep*, but see that the earth is well packed around the seed by the press wheels, attached to the back of the drill, because by pressing the surface the necessary moisture for germinating in a dry season is drawn by capillary attraction out of the deeper soil. The heavier the soil and the earlier the planting, the shallower must the sowing be in order to prevent the seed from rotting in the ground. The deeper the seed is planted, especially in heavy soil, the weaker the plants will be if they come up at all. *Therefore avoid deep planting.*

Parties growing a large acreage and not having very much help, will do well to plant the crop in sections, at intervals of one week apart, in order to gain more time for thinning; however, do not plant too late, for in that case the beets will not be strong enough when the dry season sets in, about the middle of July, and will therefore suffer from the drouth, while the earlier, and consequently stronger plants, will thrive well and a heavier and better crop be insured. *You had much better hire help during thinning time* than to plant too late.

CULTIVATING.

This work is performed with one-horse cultivators, which work two or four rows at a time. If, after sowing, a heavy rain should cause a crust to form on the field,

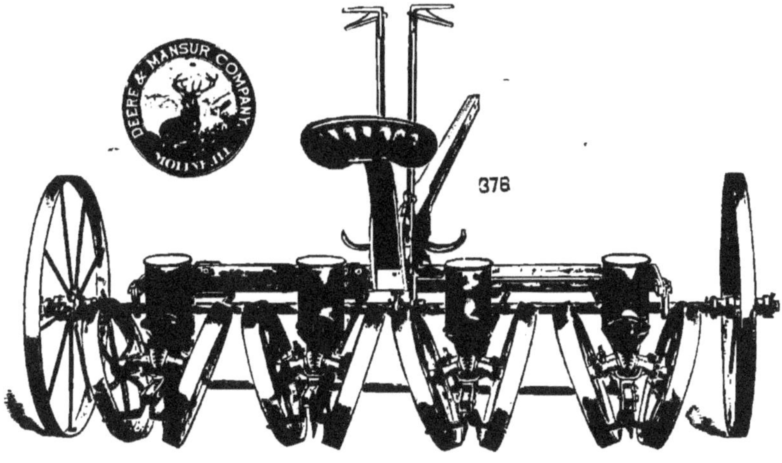

BEET DRILL.

the light harrow is recommended; but this only in case the seed has not germinated, as otherwise it would be better to run the cultivator over the field, following the rows, which can be done easily before the seed is up as the marks of the press-wheels can be plainly distinguished. *This work, however, can be better done by hand hoes* (11 inches wide; see hoeing). As soon as the beets break through the ground and the rows can be followed the cultivation *must* begin, *the earlier the better*, not only to destroy the weeds but to loosen the soil, which permits the air to penetrate, thus forcing the growth of the beet and improving its quality. It is very important *to kill the weeds before they get above the ground*, or at least before they become well-rooted. This can be easily accomplished by cultivating the field with the flat shovels every 8 to 10 days, care being taken to set the knives as close as possible to the rows, and never over two inches from the rows, as long as the beets are small. As the beets grow older, however, the shovels should be run gradually farther away from the beets, and also deeper until the leaves meet in the center of the rows, by which time the cultivation should have reached a depth of 6 inches and should then cease as the beets are ready to lay by. Besides destroying the weeds this repeated cultivation prevents evaporation from the deeper soil and secures a good and healthy growth; *Never hill your beets*, as level land keeps the moisture best.

THINNING OUT.

Care should be exercised in doing this part of the work as it is the most important of all the cultivation and care of the crop, It is very necessary that this should be done just at the right time, and the sooner it is done the better for the growth and yield of the crop. As soon as the beets have four leaves they should be thinned and must not remain longer than one week without thinning, as the roots will entwine around each other, if left longer, and make the thinning detrimental to the plant that is left. To peform this work, *the beets should be bunched* (*directly after a horse*

FOUR-ROW CULTIVATOR.

cultivator) *with an ordinary 6 inch hoe, cutting six inches of beets out and leaving a two-inch bunch containing from 3 to 6 beets.* After the beets are bunched the healthiest plant in each bunch is selected by the thinner to be left standing, the others being pulled out by hand, together with all the weeds near by. This operation will leave one plant every nine or ten inches *and the ground should be pushed up well around each* (but not packed).

HOEING.

The first hoeing, which is very important for the growth of the small plants, must be given with an ordinary 11 inch hoe between the rows of 1½ to 2 inches deep and as soon as the beets break through the ground, or if crust is formed, as soon as this occurs, following the press-wheel marks.

As the ground will have become packed during the bunching and thinning, thus

I. Thinning Beets.

preventing proper circulation of air, and the young plants, moreover, will have become weakened by their disturbance; and for the further reason that it is cheaper to do it then, the second hoeing should be given with a 7 inch hoe the day after the beets are thinned, and never later than a few days after, care being taken to kill the weeds out close to the plant but in such a manner as not to loosen or injure the beets. As the cultivator only loosens and clears the ground between the rows, the hoe must perform this work between the different plants. This hoeing should be three inches deep. A similar hoeing may be necessary twice after this, the last depending upon the freedom from weeds, also upon whether the ground is loose enough to enable the roots to grow. Both of the last hoeings should be as deep as it is possible to make

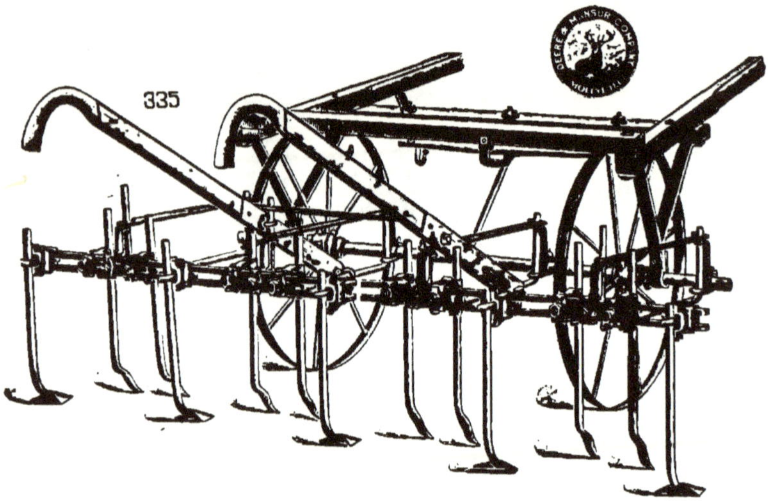

FOUR ROW CULTIVATOR.

them without injuring or loosening the plant. Under ordinary circumstances no work should be necessary in the field after eighty days from the time of planting except the final and deepest horse cultivation.

HARVESTING.

By the first part of October the beets are ready to harvest; the first planting generally a few weeks earlier. As the beets increase in tonnage mostly in September and the first part of October the harvesting with full force should not be started before the middle of October. The harvesting is done with a two-horse puller which loosens the beets but leaves them in the ground. After this the beets have to be pulled by hand and topped with a corn-knife at the base of the bottom leaf and can then be shipped to the factory, or siloed at the field and shipped later, after the beet-growers have finished their other farm work.

SILOING.

As to the best method of doing this, from our five years' experience in siloing in this state, we should recommend the following plan:

In the first place do not harvest your beets until they are ripe, as green beets do not keep as well in siloes as ripe ones, and besides should you harvest when too green they might not contain the necessary 12 per cent. of sugar with purity of 80 per cent.

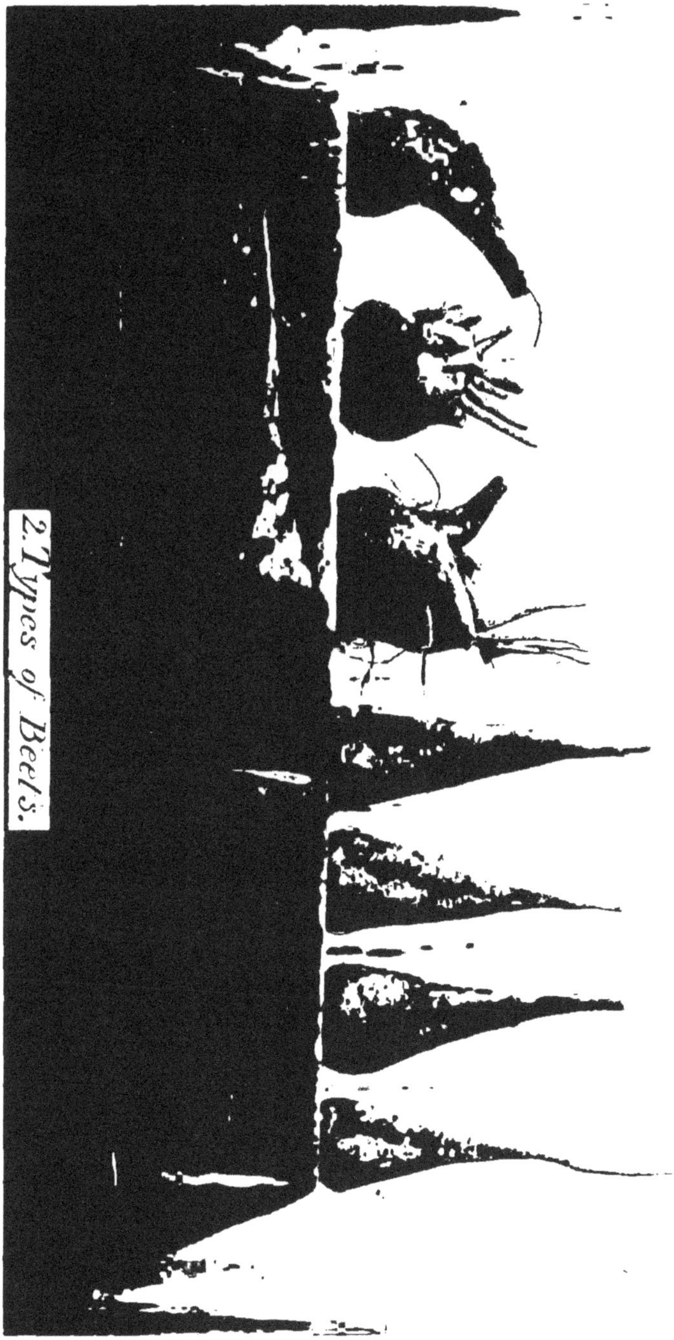

2. Types of Beets.

In an average season no beets should be siloed before October 15th, and if the weather is warm it would be better to wait until the 20th, but in no case should the beets be allowed to remain unharvested—and not siloed—until the ground freezes.

BEET LIFTER.

Frost-bitten beets will not keep; therefore all beets that you silo must be free from frost and bé covered up the same day that they are harvested.

We would advise making five to seven silos to the acre, placing not less than two tons in each silo.

When ready to silo lift the beets from forty to forty five rows with a horse harvester. These loosened beets must then be pulled out of the ground by hand and thrown in piles. It is advisable, in case the strip you have lifted contains forty-five rows, to make a pile (silo) every six rods the length of the strip, and as this section of the forty-five rows is about four rods wide and six rods long, each silo would thus contain the beets from twenty-four square rods (about one-seventh of one acre). To prevent unnecessary handling it is advisable to first pull out the beets from the middle of the marked twenty-four square rods, placing them in such shape as to make a vacant place in the center of about one rod wide and two rods long, then to pull the balance of the beets throwing them into a windrow close to and surrounding this vacant spot. When this is finished, top the beets (at the base of the bottom leaves) with one stroke of the knife and throw them in the vacant place, making a pile four feet wide and not over three feet high, the length of the pile depending entirely on the yield. After all the beets are topped and piled up in proper shape cover the pile with six inches of dirt, being careful not to have any leaves or straw on the beets or mixed with them, and also to leave wide open a hole one foot in diameter, every five feet on top of the pile (at least two in each pile) for ventilation, as beets will sweat some after siloing.

It is generally advisable not to put much more than six inches of dirt over the beets in October, but to keep them free from frost you should cover the silo before the weather gets cold, say about ten days or two weeks after harvesting, in any case, before hard frost sets in—evenly, with five to six inches of loose straw, leaving the ventilation holes uncovered, and place about two inches of dirt on top of the straw to

3. Car Silos.

prevent it from blowing away and for the purpose of packing it, as when well packed it will best keep the cold air out of the silo.

Thus the covering in the end will be composed of six inches of dirt, two inches of packed straw and then two inches more dirt.

4. Wagon Silos.

In an ordinary season such covering should keep your beets from freezing. but should there be exceptionally cold weather you might find it necessary (in case we have not ordered all your beets delivered to the factory by that time) to cover the remaining piles with some long manure.

5. Inside of Silo.

As soon as the covering of silo freezes two inches, shut the ventilation holes with dirt and then keep them shut.

GENERAL.

When beets arrive at the factory an average fifty pounds is taken from each load. They are then thoroughly washed and examined to see if properly topped, then weighed again, the loss determining the tare.

Beets can be delivered on cars at any station along the line of railroads running into Grand Island, said cars to be loaded to *their visible capacity*. The factory will make a deduction for freight as follows: Thirty cents per ton for distances of twenty-five miles from Grand Island, or under; fifty cents per ton for distances exceeding twenty-five miles and under forty-five; and for distances exceeding forty-five miles and under one hundred, eighty cents per ton. When beets are shipped from a greater distance, rates will be named on applying to the factory.

Avoid placing leaves, straw or dirt in the cars, as these are deducted from the weight of load at factory, besides which freight must be paid upon them also. It is to the farmers' interest to fill and forward the cars as rapidly as possible. Shipping tags (which will be furnished by the factory in the fall) should be tacked securely on the side of every car. When a car is sent to the factory the number and initial of same must be mailed us immediately, on a postal card.

From the foregoing any farmer can obtain a general idea of the manner in which the beet crop must be handled. In raising sugar beets it is absolutely necessary to get rid of the idea of trying to save necessary labor. Sugar beets need much work, but they pay double or treble as much as any other crop in this state, if worked well. Our six years experience has shown us that seven tons of beets per acre pay for all the team work (30 cents per hour), all the hand labor (7½ to 15 cents per hour) performed on the field, also for seed, rent of land, machinery and freight; *all of the yield above this tonnage being clear profit*. Ten tons may be regarded as an average crop per acre, although much higher yields are made. A good farmer who takes the right care of the crop and selects proper land should, in an average season, raise not less than twelve tons per acre. Our old beet growers even claim to be able to raise, in a good season, by using richly manured bottom land, 25 to 30 tons per acre, which yield has already been obtained by several parties.

The seed which is purchased by us from the most reliable growers in Europe, and is of the best varieties, will be furnished to our contractors at a nominal price and to parties not within a radius of one hundred miles of the factory we will sell the seed in small quantities (for experimental purposes), as long as we have it to spare, at twenty cents per pound cash f. o. b. Grand Island.

OXNARD BEET SUGAR COMPANY,
Grand Island and Norfolk, Neb.

LABOR.

The majority of farmers grow from 5 to 15 acres of beets and perform most of the labor themselves. It is frequently necessary, however, to hire extra help during the thinning and harvesting periods. Farmers growing more than 15 acres generally contract in the spring with one or more laborers to do the thinning, hoeing, and topping at a cost varying from $10 to $13.

While there is demand for considerable labor, yet no great difficulty has been experienced in securing help in the communities where the industry has been established. It is the opinion of those most familiar with beet culture in this country that the industry will bring with it the necessary labor.

Highly Bred Seed Essential.

The high per cent. of sugar content necessary to success in the sugar beet industry can be maintained only by the most careful methods of plant breeding. The sugar content has been increased from the four to six per cent. of the unimproved beet, to twelve and sixteen per cent. for the field crop, with individual beets testing twenty and even twenty-two per cent. of sugar. It is these last that are selected for seed production. High bred plants, like high bred animals, tend to degenerate or return to their normal condition. Especially is this true if the conditions are unfavorable and the characteristics are newly acquired, and not strongly fixed. Hence it is that the grower gives special attention to the source of his seed. He must have well bred seeds—that is, seeds with a good pedigree.

How the Seed is Produced.

The process is something as follows: The field of beets grown for this purpose is harvested with more than ordinary care to prevent any possible injury to the beets. From these the grower selects roots of good shape weighing from sixteen to twenty-five ounces, and these are stored in the silo until spring, when they are again sorted, and what are known as the "mother beets" are selected for planting. The selection is made by cutting off the tips of the roots and throwing them into a solution of common salt having a definite specific gravity, or the whole beets may be thrown in. Those which float are thrown out. Only those which sink are subjected to the final test. A hole is bored obliquely through the center of the upper portion of the beet and the juice from the pulp thus removed is tested with a polariscope, and only those containing the highest per cent of sugar are saved for planting. They are then set out in rows about thirty inches apart each way. The earth is firmly packed around the roots, and an inch of loose soil covers the crown.

In the fall the seed is harvested, cleaned, and stored in a dry place. This seed is not placed on the market, but is planted in the spring, and from this crop "mother beets" are again carefully selected and placed in the silo. In the spring following, the beets are planted as before, but the mothers are not generally subjected to the same rigid test of the polariscope.

The seed from this crop is then placed on the market. It will thus be seen that four years of work is required to produce a crop of seed for the market. The breeding of sugar beet seed is carried on extensively in Europe, but only to a limited extent in this country.

.COST AND PROFIT IN SUGAR MAKING.

The mean cost of manufacture of beet sugar in 113 German factories for the campaign of 1889 and 1890 was as follows, the figures given below being on the basis of one ton of beets:

Mean capital invested in each factory		*$193,400.00
Mean cost of beets		4.44
Salaries		.23
Labor		.66
Interest on investment		.33
Coal		.57
Miscellaneous expenses		.87
Total expense of manufacture	$	7.10
Total receipts for sugar, molasses and pulp		10.07
Profit per ton of beets	$	2.97
The mean net profit for each factory was	$	34,240 00

The following upon the cost of sugar production in the United States is quoted from Mr. Larkander, who has had extensive experience in both Europe and the United States:

DAILY EXPENSES.

(Per ton of 2,000 lb. of beets.)

Fuel (12 per cent. of weight of beets) coal @ $2.25 per ton	$ .27
Wages	.65
Lime rock (8 per cent.) @ $1.60 per ton	.13
Coke, rubber tubing, leather, filter bags, oil fat, electric light, sundry factory materials, chemical laboratory, finished goods, (bags, boxes, paper, labels, and twine) commission of agents, excluding freight for marketable sugar	.75
One ton of beets	4.00
Beet expenses	.30
Total	$6.10

ANNUAL EXPENSES.

General expenses for office, traveling and incidental expenses, salary of officers, repairing of building, including all material for the same, and pay for engineer, blacksmith, bricklayers, carpenters, etc., taxes, state, county, and city, insurance on buildings, machinery and stock, interest and discount for spot cash payments, exchange, excluding interest on shares, bonds, and mortgages	$50,000.00

*The cost of erecting similar factories in this country would be about 50 per cent. more than this. The Grand Island factory cost $350,000 and the Norfolk factory considerably exceeded this amount.

These $50,000 of general annual expenses are brought into account without regard to whether the quantity of beets handled be 40,000 or 60,000 tons per season, because the fluctuations in the expense item up or down are not great in relation to the quantity of beets.

6. Diffusion Tanks.

The value of the residue, on pulp and molasses, viz.: 1,200 pounds of pulp and 40 pounds of molasses, has been taken into calculation at the lowest market price for cattle and sheep food at 50 cents per ton of beets which is only half the value that this residue really possesses for cattle raisers or feeders.

7. Carbonation Tanks.

If the price of coal be advanced $1.00 from 2.56 per ton, then the cost of producing a pound of sugar will increase but 5-100ths of a per cent., which is too little to need consideration. More important will be the consumption of 25 per cent. or more, instead of 12 per cent. as is commonly estimated. For wages, I have estimated three times those paid in Europe, and the season's expenses ($50,000) are estimated at least 50 per cent. higher than is estimated in good running European factories. The same principle has been followed in the estimate of 75 cents per ton in daily expenses for various necessary articles.

We reach the conclusion that a factory using annually 40,000 to 50,000 tons of beets, and producing 180 to 220 pounds of granulated sugar from each ton of beets produces a pound of sugar at a cost of 3¼ cents.

The selling price of sugar will be materially higher later, when raw sugar is bought at Hamburg or Cuba and imported under the present Dingley tariff, for the cost of granulated sugar made from imported raw sugar, refined in the United States today is surely 5½ cents and higher per pound, against about 3½ cents for granulated sugar produced from beets grown in the United States. Therefore, I predict that the beet sugar industry will grow and prosper in this country.

* *Where the Money Goes.*—The Chicago Inter-Ocean, investigating the Lehi, Utah, sugar factory operations for the year 1893†, reports the expenses of the factory for various items to be as follows:

28,800 tons of beets which cost	$142,233.96
4,500 tons of coal at $3	13,500.00
200 tons of coke at $17.10	3,420.00
1,600 tons of lime rock at $2.50	4,022.50
40,000 double sugar bags at 14½c	5,800.00
4,150 yards of heavy duck at 15c	622.50
1,050 yards of German duck at 50c	525.00
6,000 pounds of sal soda	150.00
4,500 pounds of tallow	270.00
30,000 pounds of sulphur	600.00
10,000 pounds of muriatic acid	350.00
Laboratory and other supplies	5,000.06
Paid for labor	52,923.80
	$230,417.64

The following letter is from James G. Hamilton, Vice-President Oxnard Construction Company, in reply to an invitation to be in attendance at the Sugar Beet Convention to be held at the University, beginning February 25th:

NEW YORK, January 21, 1898.

E. Davenport, Esq.,
Urbana, Ill.

DEAR SIR:—Replying to yours of the 10th inst. would state that we appreciate the good work which you are doing in showing to the public the inadvisability of going recklessly into the erection of beet sugar plants and we should be glad to be present at the meeting on February 25th that you speak of, but are so occupied with the erection of a large plant in Southern California, that such would be impossible.

This company has been organized with the view of not only building and equipping beet or cane sugar plants for those desiring to go into the business, but also for manning and where necessary running the plant for its first campaign.

*Wis. Bull. No. 55 †Capacity trebled since 1893.

You are probably aware that we have built and are operating three of the most successful factories in this country and should the policy of our national government be that of protection to the sugar industry of the United States, there is no reason why in a comparatively short period of time, we should not produce all the sugar consumed by our citizens. * * * Yours very truly,

OXNARD CONSTRUCTION CO.,
J. G. HAMILTON,
Vice-President.

At the request of the Experiment Station the American Copper, Brass & Iron Works, Chicago, furnishes the following valuable communication relative to the cost of erecting factories, and the conditions necessary for their successful operation:

CHICAGO, Jan. 21, 1898.

The cost of a beet sugar factory depends greatly upon the completeness of its installation; much contradictory advice is given on this subject by various parties, who have sprung up all over our country as experts and promoters, in the hopes of reaping a harvest out of the coming boom in the sugar business.

To build sugar factories it takes large capital and the agreement of the surrounding farmer community to supply the necessary beets for operating the same. A sugar factory without beets or beets without a factory cannot exist, but both interests must be identical. The farmer or beet grower must first encourage capital with his willingness to enter into contracts for a number of years, not one, two or three years, but five years or more, so as to satisfy the parties who will furnish the money for erecting the factory that they need not fear for want of supply of the product necessary to operate such an institution and thus insure the investment made by the capitalist. The better and surer way would be for the beet raisers themselves to aid such an enterprise financially and thus become more closely identified with the success of the factory. If capital can be convinced that the before mentioned conditions can be accomplished there will be no trouble of obtaining the necessary means for erecting factories.

The success of beet sugar making in the United States has been fully demonstrated by the results obtained by the few up-to-date factories now in operation. This is due to no cheap concerns, but to establishments which are in every respect strictly complete and equipped with the very best up-to-date machinery and arrangements, built according to practical experience and scientific researches, and especially those designed and erected by American engineers and equipped with American machinery and by reputable manufacturers of such machinery.

The cost of such machinery is so varied that it is almost impossible to give an approximation of the cost of same owing to the different constructions and qualifications. The most experienced and reputable contractors and manufacturers give the figures of a plant all complete and ready to operate, equipped with the very best and modern machinery and buildings and the most approved arrangements at $1,000.00 for each ton of beets which such a factory will consume in 24 hours. That is, a factory of 350 tons would cost $350,000.00.

This estimate is substantially correct, but much depends on the location, foundations for buildings, water supply, cost of building material, freight rates, etc., which cannot very well be given in a general approximation.

Sugar factories are most always contracted for complete with buildings, beet sheds, water intake and the entire equipments ready to operate; or the complete machinery equipment without buildings; but in the latter case the plans must be furnished by the machinery contractor so as to adapt them to the machinery to be installed in same, which is very heavy and bulky, and requires a well calculated and strong, substantial structure.

No factory should be built by piecemeal, that is machinery procured from various manufacturers and erected by parties who may attempt to build sugar factories in that way, for the reason that all the machinery must harmonize and be proportioned together, if it is to be successful. In this way of building no one will want to assume responsibility in case of failure of any of the apparatuses, and it may cause serious delays and great damage to the company. Delays and break-downs mean the loss of the beet crop which will have to be paid for by the company whether utilized or not.

Buildings for sugar factories should always be designed large enough and with the view that the capacity can be increased or doubled at any future time. The extra outlay for this in the beginning is not very much more, and will be found greatly advantageous in the future. The extra help required in a factory of double capacity is proportionally smaller than when two separate factories are operated. Labor is a great and costly factor, and therefore only the most improved labor-saving arrangements should be employed, designed by experienced and practical engineers who understand the wants and requirements of a successful sugar factory.

These suggestions are conscientiously made in the hopes that they may assist in promoting the beet sugar interest in our state, and to prevent any existing misconceptions among the readers of your valued bulletin. The writer has had many years' practical experience in designing and erecting sugar factories and sugar machinery, and has been prominently connected in assisting in the designing of the Lehi, Utah, sugar factory, and as superintendent of erecting the machinery of that plant.

J. NEUERT, M. E. Supt.,

American Copper, Brass & Iron Works.

Sugar Machinery Department.

Acreage Necessary to Supply a Factory.

From 3,500 to 4,500 acres will be required to supply the average sized factory with 40 to 50 thousand tons of beets for a campaign. At Grand Island and Norfolk about three-fifths of the beets are produced within a radius of eight miles of the factories, or hauling distance. The other two-fifths are produced outside of this radius and shipped in by rail, in some instances a distance of 85 miles.

There are 128,500 acres within a radius of 8 miles. If, therefore, all the beets necessary to supply a factory were grown within this area, less than three of every eighty acres would be required, or about 3 per cent.

STATISTICS—LITERATURE—MACHINERY.

The following tables furnish much valuable information relative to the beet sugar industry both in Europe and in the United States:

WORLD'S CONSUMPTION OF SUGAR.*

Country.	1896. Total amount in tons.	1895. Pounds per capita.
United States	1,960,000	62.60
Canada and Provinces	140,000	....
Great Britain	1,494,000	86.09
Germany	594,000	26.78
Austria	343,000	19.81
Holland and Belgium	391,000	....
France	555,000	30.62
Russia	500,000	10.94
Other countries of Europe (estimated)	513,000	....
	6,490,000	....
Unaccounted for	1,347,000	....
Total production	7,837,000	....

* Edwin F. Atkins in FORUM for Nov., 1897.

GROWTH OF THE BEET SUGAR INDUSTRY.

France.		Germany.		United States.	
Year.	Tons of sugar.	Year.	Tons of sugar.	Year.	Tons of sugar.
1830	4,000	1840	12,000	1887	310
1840	22,000	1850	52,000	1890	4,000
1850	62,000	1860	126,000	1891	6,000
1860	126,000	1865	180,000	1892	6,003
1870	282,000	1870	186,000	1893	13,542
1873	410,000	1880	599,000	1894	22,555
1890	750,000	1890	1,200,000	1895	33,600
1896	750,000	1896	1,845,000	1897	40,000

NUMBER OF FACTORIES, YIELD OF BEETS PER ACRE, AND YIELD OF SUGAR IN THE PRINCIPAL BEET SUGAR COUNTRIES OF THE WORLD, 1895–96.

GERMANY.—The number of factories, 397; quantity of beets used, 10,589,413 tons; number of acres cultivated, 930,372; mean yield per acre, 13.8 tons; mean price of beets, $4.64 per ton; yield of raw sugar, 13.11 per cent. on weight of beets; average output of raw sugar per factory, 3,690 tons.

FRANCE.—Number of factories, 356; quantity of beets used, 4,909,221 tons; yield of refined sugar, 10.97 per cent. on weight of beets; number of acres cultivated, 405,852; yield of beets, 9.5 tons per acre; average output of refined sugar per factory, 1,702 tons.

AUSTRIA-HUNGARY.—Number of factories, 216; quantity of beets used, 5,225,390 tons; yield of raw sugar, 13.5 per cent. on weight of beets; average output of raw sugar from each factory, 3,323 tons.

RUSSIA.—Number of factories, 273; quantity of beets used, 4,818,869 tons; per cent. of raw sugar in beets, 15.71; average output of sugar for each factory, 2,565 tons.

FACTORIES IN OTHER COUNTRIES:—*Belgium*, 121; *Holland*, 30; *Spain*, 15; *Sweden*, 10; *United States*, 7; *Scotland*, 50.

NUMBER OF FACTORIES OPERATING IN 1895-6.

Germany	397
France	356
Russia	273
Austria Hungary	216
Belgium	121
Holland	30
Spain	15
Sweden	10
United States	7
Scattered	50
Total	1,475

EXPORT BOUNTIES PAID IN 1894 TO SUGAR FACTORIES.

Germany	$ 5,781,250	Austria Hungary	$2,000,000
France	10,000,000	Belgium	5,000,000

VALUE OF THE SUGAR AND MOLASSES IMPORTED INTO THE UNITED STATES, AND OF THE WHEAT AND FLOUR EXPORTED FROM THE UNITED STATES 1891 TO 1895 INCLUSIVE.

	1891.	1892.	1893.	1894.	1895.	Totals 1891-5.
Imported—						
Sugar	$105,728,216	104,408,813	116,255,784	126,871,889	76,462,838	525,727,538
Molasses	2,659,172	2,659,172	1,992,334	1,984,778	1,295,146	10,809,174
Total	$108,387,388	107,067,985	118,248,118	128,856,667	77,757,984	540,536,712
Exported—						
Wheat	$ 51,420,272	161,399,132	93,534,970	59,407,041	43,805,663	409,567,078
Wheat flour	54,705,616	75,362,283	75,494,347	69,271,770	51,651,928	326,485,944
Total	$106,125,888	236,767,415	169,029,317	128,678,711	95,457,591	736,053,022

*IMPORTS OF SUGAR INTO THE UNITED STATES FOR YEAR ENDING JUNE 30, 1896.

Country.	Value.	Country.	Value.
Austria	$ 931,263	Santo Domingo	$ 2,459,302
Belgium	1,771,977	Cuba	24,215,935
Germany	12,528,755	Puerto Rico	2,227,593
Holland	1,182,605	Phillipine Islands	2,270,902
Dutch East Indies	11,388,487	Brazil	3,776,487
Dutch Guiana	289,243	Hawaiian Islands	11,338,698
British West Indies	4,758,569		
British Guiana	3,414,368	Total	$82,554,183

*Edwin F. Atkins in FORUM for Nov., 1897.

*CONDENSED DATA CONCERNING THE BEET SUGAR INDUSTRY OF GERMANY.

	1894-5.	1893-4.	1892-3.
Factories working	405	405	401
Number of steam engines	5,324	5,256	5,122
Total horse power	94,952	87,424	81,596
Total beets worked (tons)	14,526,030	10,644,352	9,811,940
Total area devoted to beets (acres)	1,098,465	987,723	880,000
Average yield of beets per acre (tons)	12.8	10 9	11.7
Raw sugar extracted.	Tons.	Tons.	Tons.
From beets in factories	1,769,331	1,319,006	1,175,137
From molasses (special factories)	61,447	55,165	48,925
From molasses in refineries	4,396	1,427	500
Total raw sugar	1,835,174	1,375,598	1,224,562
Per cent. extracted from beets worked	12.17	12.36	11.98
Per cent. extraction, including the working of molasses	12.64	12.92	12.48
Yield of sugar per acre (lb.)	3,514	3,149	3,276
Weight of beets required to produce 100 lb. raw sugar (lb.)	822	809	835
Molasses per 100 lb. beets worked	2.4	2.63	2.54
Total molasses extracted (tons)	347,125	279,757	246,272
Consumption of sugar per capita (lb.)	23.5	20.2	21.8

* Wis. Bull. No. 55.

RESULTS OBTAINED BY TWO AMERICAN BEET SUGAR FACTORIES DURING FIVE YEARS.

Factory at Lehi, South of Salt Lake City, Utah.

	1891.	1892.	1893.	1894.	1895.
Acres of beets grown	1,500	1,500	2,755	2,850	3,300
Tons of beets produced	9,960	9,816	26,800	32,694	38,108
Average yield of beets per acre (tons)	6.6	6.5	9.7	11.47	11.54
Per cent. of sugar in beets	11.0	11.8	11.6	12.7	13.5
Purity of sugar per cent	80.0	80.0	79.5	80.2	81.5
Crude sugar per acre (lb.)	1,452	1,534	2,250	2,913	3,116
Pure sugar per acre (lb.)	1,162	1,227	1,719	2,336	2,539
Began making sugar	Oct. 12	Sept. 26	Sept. 19	Sept. 25	Sept. 5
Finishing making sugar	Dec. 8	Nov. 13	Dec. 21	Jan. 5	Dec. 31
Days in operation	58	49	94	103	118

Chino, California, Beet Sugar Company.

	1891.	1892.	1893.	1894.	1895.
Acres of beets grown	1,800	3,488	4,191	4,778	7,529
Tons of beets produced	13,080	26,266	49,353	43,773	83,035
Average yield of beets per acre (tons)	7.26	7.50	11.7	9.16	11.03
Per cent. of sugar in beets	13	14	14	15	15
Crude sugar per acre (lb.)	1,888	2,100	3,276	2,748	3,309
Sugar per acre 80 per cent. pure	1,510	1,680	2,621	2,198	2,670
Began making sugar	Aug. 20	July 13	July 31	Aug. 2	July 9
Finished making sugar	Oct. 31	Oct. 11	Nov. 4	Oct. 24	Nov. 14
Days in operation	73	91	97	85	129
Average weight of beets worked daily (tons)	179	288	509	526	644
Average weight of sugar made daily (lb.)	28,108	86,852	15,592	111,431	161,129
Total weight of sugar made (tons)	1,026	3,952	7,532	4,736	10,393
Average price paid farmers per ton, beets.	$3.90	$4.26	$4.26	$4.66	$4.35
Average return per acre	$28.37	$31.95	$49.84	$42.69	$47.98

Wis. Bull. No. 55.

* Pounds of sugar per ton of beets:—The tonnage of beets worked up at the Norfolk, Neb., sugar factory for the past five years, and the yield of sugar per ton of beets for the same period, are as follows:

Year.	Tons of beets.	Pounds of sugar.	Pounds of sugar per ton.
1891	8,183	1,318,700	161
1892	10,725	1,698,400	157
1893	22,625	4,107,300	181.5
1894	25,633	6,000,000	218
1895	27,204	4,991,300	183.4

*Wis. Bull. No. 55.

SUGAR BEET LITERATURE.

United States Department of Agriculture,—Special Report No. 28, (300 pages). A report on the culture of the sugar beet and the manufacture of sugar therefrom in the United States and France.

United States Department of Agriculture,—Farmer's Bulletin No. 52 (1897).

United States Department of Agriculture, Division of Chemistry,—The Sugar Beet Industry, Bulletin No. 27 (262 pages).

Agricultural Experiment Station, Lincoln, Neb.,—Bulletins 13, 16, 27, 36, 38 and 44.

Agricultural Experiment Station, Madison, Wis.,—Bulletin No. 55.

Most, if not all the above publications can be had free by writing the United States Department of Agriculture, Washington, D. C., or the respective Experiment Stations.

The Sugar Beet, by L. S. Ware, contains 320 pages. It includes a history of the industry in Europe, study of soils, tillage, seeds, and sowing, yields and cost of cultivation, harvesting, transportation, feeding value of pulp, etc.

["The author spent fourteen years in Europe, studying the subject, the aim of his work being to induce American farmers to cultivate the sugar beet for extraction of sugar. The work amounts in fact to a handbook on the subject, and is the best of its kind in the English language. It is most thorough from beginning to end, giving the fullest details in every particular."—H. L. Roth.] Henry Carey Baird & Co., 810 Walnut St., Philadelphia.

Whatever other publications are consulted the community should provide itself at the outset with a standard periodical devoted exclusively to the industry, such as THE SUGAR BEET, Philadelphia, a monthly, edited by L. S. Ware, author of the book above mentioned. Price, $1 per year.

SPECIAL MACHINERY.

In addition to the ordinary farm machinery there will be required a beet seeder ($40 to $50), a cultivator ($25 to $35), and a lifter ($6 to $8).

The following companies manufacture standard sugar beet machinery, cuts of which appear in these pages:

Deere & Mansur Company, Moline, Illinois.

Moline Plow Company, Moline, Illinois.

Superior Drill Company, Springfield, Ohio.

For references to construction companies and beet sugar machinery consult "The Sugar Beet," the monthly mentioned above.

PERRY G. HOLDEN, M. S.,
Assistant Agriculturist.

CYRIL G. HOPKINS, M. S.,
Chemist.

www.ingramcontent.com/pod-product-compliance
Lightning Source LLC
Chambersburg PA
CBHW031809090426
42739CB00008B/1223
* 9 7 8 3 3 3 7 1 3 0 7 0 1 *